MDA Distilled

MDA Distilled

Principles of Model-Driven Architecture

Stephen J. Mellor
Kendall Scott
Axel Uhl
Dirk Weise

✦Addison-Wesley

Boston • San Francisco • New York • Toronto • Montreal
London • Munich • Paris • Madrid
Capetown • Sydney • Tokyo • Singapore • Mexico City

Many of the designations used by manufacturers and sellers to distinguish their products are claimed as trademarks. Where those designations appear in this book, and Addison-Wesley was aware of a trademark claim, the designations have been printed with initial capital letters or in all capitals.

The authors and publisher have taken care in the preparation of this book, but make no expressed or implied warranty of any kind and assume no responsibility for errors or omissions. No liability is assumed for incidental or consequential damages in connection with or arising out of the use of the information or programs contained herein.

The publisher offers discounts on this book when ordered in quantity for bulk purchases and special sales. For more information, please contact:

U.S. Corporate and Government Sales
(800) 382-3419
corpsales@pearsontechgroup.com

For sales outside of the U.S., please contact:

International Sales
(317) 581-3793
international@pearsontechgroup.com

Visit Addison-Wesley on the Web: www.awprofessional.com

Library of Congress Cataloging-in-Publication Data
MDA Distilled: Principles of model-driven architecture / Stephen J.Mellor ... [et al.]
    p. cm.
 Includes bibliographical references and index.
 ISBN 0-201-78891-8 (pbk. : alk. paper)
 1. Computer software--Development. 2. Computer architecture. I.
Mellor, Stephen J.

QA76.76.D47P75 2004
005.1--dc22

                            2004001765

ISBN 0-201-78891-8
Text printed on recycled paper
1 2 3 4 5 6 7 8 9 10—CRS—0807060504
First printing, March 2004

To Florian.
Du hast mein Leben verändert.
Thanks heaps mate.

— Steve

To Jennifer Garner
(anyone who doesn't understand this just isn't paying attention).

— Kendall

To Petra and Linus.
For their love and their smiles.

— Axel

To Matka and Senior. To Andrea.

— Dirk

Contents

Figures

Foreword

It's all John Backus' fault. Before his landmark work in the 1950s, everything was so simple.

Jim Gray once noted that "In the beginning, there was FORTRAN." But of course, that wasn't the beginning. The genesis was recognition of a pair of problems. Dr. Cuthbert C. Hurd, Director of IBM's Applied Science Division, noticed in the summer of 1952 that programming the IBM Defense Calculator (later romantically renamed the IBM 701) was quite difficult. He also noticed, however, that the 701 was a speed demon: While watching leading mathematicians of the day have a try at the new machine, he has been quoted as saying, "They each got a shot at the computer. They would feed a program into the computer and, bam, you got the result…We all sat there and said, 'How are we going to keep this machine busy? It's so tremendously fast. How are we going to do that?'"

What a marvelous juxtaposition: The machine was fast as could be, and also difficult to program. In 1953, Hurd proposed that his staffer John Backus do something about this juxtaposition. The result was the Speedcoding system, developed in 1954, and released to the world in 1957 as the FORmula TRANslation system, or FORTRAN for short. Today we don't think much about compilation; it's a fact of life, and we have a plethora of languages from which to choose, each theoretically tuned to some class of problems or infrastructure. But in fact FORTRAN was a critically important first step, the greatest remove yet (in 1957) from the machine's own representation of programs.

Since then, we have apparently flown up the abstraction ladder. Later languages let the programmer pretend infinite memory via automatic memory management (Lisp, for example, or Basic); or bizarre execution models (Prolog or MICROPLANNER being obvious examples). In each case, programmer productivity soared, sometimes (but not always) with attendant increase in run-time cost in space and time.

It's notable, however, that the original FORTRAN system produced excellent code. A member of Backus' own team, Harlan Herrick, remembered in 1982, "I said, 'John, we can't possibly simulate a human programmer with a language—this language—that would produce machine code that would even approach the efficiency of a human programmer like me, for example. I'm a great programmer, don't you know?'" Nevertheless, the cover of 1956's *Fortran Automatic Coding System for the IBM 704* proudly states, "Object Programs produced by Fortran will be nearly as efficient as those written by good programmers." Somehow the high-level abstraction allowed by programming languages does not always have significant run-time costs, so long as the precision of the abstraction allows complete definition of the algorithm.

And so abstraction has marched on. In fact this "compilation" idea is quite well-understood today: What a compiler (or interpreter or assembler, for that matter) does is to translate one model of an algorithm into another (presumably "lower-level") model of the same algorithm. Now if we could just allow the capture of algorithms in some language that feels closer to the mathematical or structural formalisms natural to those who develop the algorithms, and also ensure that mappings exist from those high-level formalisms to the low-level formalisms our real computers understand (i.e., machine language)!

This, in essence, is the promise of Model Driven Architecture (MDA). By asking developers to use precise but abstract and graphical representations of algorithms, MDA allows the construction of computing systems from models that can be understood much more quickly and deeply than can programming language "code." Coding languages—even "high-level" languages like Smalltalk and Lisp—overlay many unintentional constraints and structural styles over the specification of an algorithm. Modeling languages, in contrast, while certainly overlaying a style and structure, attempt not to constrain the expression of the algorithm, which allows extra freedoms to the compiler and much more clarity of expression to the developer—and more importantly, to the maintainer who must figure out the underlying algorithm in order to correct bugs or integrate an existing system with something new.

Not that this leap is a trivial one, of course. Thankfully, MDA doesn't expect that leap of abstraction (and of faith!) to be taken all at once. While it is certainly worth some investment, some "activation energy" to reduce the immense costs of software development, maintenance, and integration, one must expect some expense to shift to a higher abstraction view. You hold in your hands a first step, a distillation of the thoughts and technique that comprise a complete and comprehensive approach to building, maintaining, and integrating software systems using a Model Driven Architecture approach.

The *Oxford English Dictionary* advises us that in the 14th century, the new word "distill" came to mean, "To trickle down or fall in minute drops..." Sometimes learning a new technology is unfortunately more like drinking from a fire hose. In this book, you are offered a step-by-step distillation (in the Oxford sense, "gentle dropping or falling," we hope!) of the techniques that will make you successful in building software better, faster, and cheaper. Layering on the abstractions one at a time, the authors take you through the modeling steps to succeed with this approach to building reliable, maintainable, and integratable systems.

One of my favorite authors, Chaim Potok, wrote, "All beginnings are hard." Though he may not have been thinking of MDA at the time, he also added a character note, "Then the drawing tells me what I'm trying to say." May your drawings tell you—and those who must interpret your work—what you are you trying to say.

Richard Mark Soley, Ph.D.
Lexington, Massachusetts
December 2003

Preface

In 2000, the Object Management Group (OMG) published "Model Driven Architecture" (OMG 2000), a white paper that described a vision for software development that relied on linking object models together to build complete systems. This **model-driven architecture** (**MDA**) approach would employ existing technologies that support existing and future OMG standards, and thereby support model-driven development so that object models would become assets instead of expenses.

Today, however, models are precisely that: They're expenses. Once a model has been built, it must be transformed into code, and this is a tedious, error-prone, and above all, expensive process. Furthermore, once the interesting abstraction work has been done, only the transformation from code to an executable is automated. Once again, we find that the cobblers' children have no shoes.

MDA is the result of the recognition that interoperability is a Good Thing and that modeling is a Good Thing, too. MDA allows developers to build models without knowledge of other models in the system and then combine those models *only at the last minute* to create the system. This prevents design decisions from becoming intertwined with the application; it also renders the application independent of its implementation so the application can be recombined with other technologies, as well as other application subject matters, at some later time. This is a kind of *design-time interoperability* of models; the result is that models become *assets*.

Does this sound too good to be true? Possibly. However, MDA doesn't require a one-step leap from a code-driven process to one driven by modeling. Instead, it offers features that allow the progressive adoption of the technology. You'll likely find that some of the technologies are in place in your organization already—MDA simply fits them together and organizes them into a coherent whole.

This book describes the current state of the art in MDA. It's targeted to developers and their managers who want to understand more fully what MDA is, and how it might affect their development activities and their organization. It's *not* intended to describe all of the nitty-gritty detail of MDA.

Organization of This Book

Chapter 1, Introduction, provides a high-level overview of MDA in terms of how it's aimed at raising the levels of abstraction and reuse. It also discusses *design-time interoperability*, which ties these ideas together into a greater whole, and the concept of models as assets.

Chapter 2, MDA Terms and Concepts, offers introductory definitions of the various acronyms and terms at the heart of MDA. It also provides a road map for the rest of the book.

Chapter 3, Building Models, explains why modeling systems is important, describes the key aspects of good models, and discusses the important concepts of abstraction, classification, and generalization. This chapter also introduces a banking system example that will run throughout the book and provides initial definitions of the terms platform-independent model (PIM) and platform-specific model (PSM).

Chapter 4, Building Metamodels, focuses on the core concepts of metamodels, which are models of modeling languages. This chapter explores the Meta-Object Facility (MOF), which is the OMG's adopted standard for metamodeling. This chapter also expands the discussion of the banking system to show the relationship between elements of the basic model and the elements of the Unified Modeling Language (UML) metamodel.

Chapter 5, Building Mappings, describes the need for mappings between models and describes some mapping functions that might apply in connection with transforming an "analysis" model to a "design" model. It also discusses various types of "horizontal" and "vertical" mappings and issues associated with merging mappings.

Chapter 6, Building Marking Models, discusses marks, which are nonintrusive extensions to models and metamodels that capture necessary information without polluting them. In particular, the focus is on what marks are good for and how to find them for a given mapping function. This chapter also defines the concept of marking models, which serve as adapters between metamodels.

Chapter 7, Building Languages, describes how to use a metamodel to define a language for the purposes of improving communication among team members and with machines. This discussion includes an exploration of two different approaches to building languages, one of which involves the MOF and the other of which involves UML profiles.

Chapter 8, Elaborating Models, addresses the idea that a model can be modified after it has been generated. This includes three topics that support MDA's open-minded attitude: managing manual changes to target models, reversibility of mappings, and, most important of all, legacy code.

Chapter 9, Building Executable Models, describes the principles behind models that have everything required to produce the desired functionality of a single domain. These models confer independence from the *software* platform, which makes them portable across multiple development environments. The chapter also discusses Executable UML, a profile of UML that defines an execution semantics for a carefully selected streamlined subset of UML.

Chapter 10, Agile MDA, discusses an approach to MDA that involves linking models together rather than transforming them, and then mapping all of these models to a single combined model that is subsequently translated into code according to a single system architecture. This approach relies on the Executable UML profile discussed in Chapter 9.

Chapter 11, Building an MDA Process, describes how to select models, mapping functions, and marking models so they fit together into a process suitable for MDA development. Topics include charting the MDA process, identifying models, identifying metamodels and marking models, and constraint propagation.

Chapter 12, Executing an MDA Process, discusses how a model-driven development process works in terms of the key activities and their interdependencies. The discussion includes descriptions of the high-level activities required for conducting any model-driven process, the issues involved in defining a specific process for a project in the presence of multiple platforms and then how to go about it, and how to implement the process and test the resulting system.

Chapter 13, The Future of MDA, describes the authors' views of the most likely directions in which the OMG will take MDA.

The book also includes a glossary, which contains definitions for all of the terms introduced in the body of the text; a bibliography; and an index.

Frequently Asked Questions

What is MDA? MDA is actually three things:

- An OMG initiative to develop standards based on the idea that modeling is a better foundation for developing and maintaining systems
- A brand for standards and products that adhere to those standards
- A set of technologies and techniques associated with those standards

What are these technologies and techniques? There are many. The most well-known is probably the UML, which people use to capture abstract semantics models as well as the software structure of object systems. Others include the following:

- The MOF, a metamodel and modeling language for describing metamodels (don't panic—we'll explain each of these terms later in the book)
- Mapping functions
- Marking models
- Executable models

It's the job of this book to explain each of these concepts and—most importantly—how they relate to one another.

Is that all? No. At present, MDA is still in development, and some of the technologies need to be developed further and standardized, while others need further definition.

If they're not defined, what good are they? The ideas behind MDA have been around for years; they're only just now in the process of formalization and standardization. For example, people have been building executable models, generating code, and refining and transforming models for some years now, and gaining significant benefits from doing so.

It takes a long time to build standards. Should I wait? No. Much of the technology has been around for a while, and you may even have been using it. It also takes time to bring a new technology into an organization, and in any case, you can do so progressively.

What is the purpose of this book? As the title indicates, it's a "distilled" discussion of MDA. We think it's the book you *have* to have to help you understand MDA and not be caught out by your colleagues.

What does the book do? It explains what MDA is, what makes it up, what each of the relevant technologies and tools is, and what their importance is in the larger context of MDA. In so doing, we also explain the benefits.

Who are the people that should read this book? Developers who are trying to get ahead of the crashing MDA wave.

I'm a manager. Should I read this book? If you need to understand how the benefits of MDA derive from the associated technologies and tools, this is the book for you. We explain technologies and tools so you can understand the benefit, but we don't just tell you why something is important—we also explain the technology.

What do I need to know to read this book? Nothing, except an acquaintance with UML.

I know all about MOF and UML. Do I need this book? Yes, if you want to know how UML and the rest fit into the larger picture. MDA relies on these technologies and takes them forward a step. We also identify those parts of these technologies that don't apply to MDA.

I'm in real-time. Does this book apply to me? The principles behind MDA apply to software development in general; they aren't specific to a certain kind of software. The ideas described here apply equally to real-time and regular IT systems; some of them, such as Executable and Translatable UML, were developed first for real-time systems.

Acknowledgments

We had a large review team. We'd like to thank Jim Arlow for rescuing you from our more tortured attempts at humor; Conrad Bock for acting as the UML Policeman (we respect his authoritay); Krzysztof Czarnecki for ensuring that we related MDA to the Generative Programming movement and providing detailed comments, some of which we lifted directly; Andy Evans for making us distinguish automated refinement from manual elaboration and otherwise keeping us honest; Joaquin Miller for his gentle (if annoyingly difficult) questions, especially in the area of metamodeling; Ulf Schreier for some high-level reorganization; Richard Soley for keeping our eyes on the ball; and John Wolfe for pointing out some high-level flaws in our arguments, and his detailed comments, some of which we also borrowed directly.

As for getting the book from concept to production, we'd like to thank Mary O'Brien, our acquisitions editor, for playing a multifaceted role, one of which involves buying lunch at Davio's; Brenda Mulligan, who resolved important details as the material was readied for publication; Lynda D'Arcangelo, our copy editor, who removed repetition, scrubbed the language one more time, removed repetition, and has a fine sense of humor (she needed it sometimes); and Elizabeth Ryan, production coordinator, who was responsible for all matters from copyedit through bound books, and who was (somehow) able to work with Kendall.

And yes, having the last word now, it was a pleasure to work with such a multicontinental team, despite the near impossibility of scheduling a teleconference.

Stephen J. Mellor
Sydney, Australia

Kendall Scott
Harrison, Tennessee

Axel Uhl
Freiburg, Germany

Dirk Weise
Freiburg, Germany

Chapter 1

Introduction

There's no doubt about it: Software is expensive. The United States alone devotes at least $250 billion each year to application development of approximately 175,000 projects involving several million people. For all of this investment of time and money, though, software's customers continue to be disappointed, because over 30 percent of the projects will be canceled before they're completed, and more than half of the projects will cost nearly twice their original estimates.[1]

The demand for software also continues to rise. The developed economies rely to a large extent on software for telecommunications, inventory control, payroll, word processing and typesetting, and an ever-widening set of applications. Only a decade ago, the Internet was text-based, known only to a relatively few scientists connected using DARPAnet and email. Nowadays, it seems as if everyone has his or her own website. Certainly, it's become difficult to conduct even non-computer-related business without email.

There's no end in sight. A Star Trek world of tiny communications devices, voice-recognition software, vast searchable databases of human (for the moment, anyway) knowledge, sophisticated computer-controlled sensing devices, and intelligent display are now imaginable. (As software

---

1. Consult sources such as Ovum (http://www.ovum.com) and the Standish Group (http://www.standishgroup.com) for more definitive numbers. Each analyst uses different criteria to establish his or her numbers.

professionals, however, we know just how much ingenuity will be required to deliver these new technologies.)

Software practitioners, industrial experts, and academics have not been idle in the face of this need to improve productivity. There have been significant improvements in the ways in which we build software over the last fifty years, two of which are worthy of note in our attempts to make software an asset. First, we've raised the level of abstraction of the languages we use to express behavior; second, we've sought to increase the level of reuse in system construction.

These techniques have undoubtedly improved productivity, but as we bring more powerful tools to bear to solve more difficult problems, the size of each problem we're expected to tackle increases to the point at which we could, once again, barely solve it.

MDA takes the ideas of raising the levels of abstraction and reuse up a notch. It also introduces a new idea that ties these ideas together into a greater whole: design-time interoperability.

Raising the Level of Abstraction[2]

The history of software development is a history of raising the level of abstraction. Our industry used to build systems by soldering wires together to form hard-wired programs. Machine code let us store programs by manipulating switches to enter each instruction. Data was stored on drums whose rotation time had to be taken into account so that the head would be able to read the next instruction at exactly the right time. Later, assemblers took on the tedious task of generating sequences of ones and zeroes from a set of mnemonics designed for each hardware platform.

At some point, programming languages, such as FORTRAN, were born and "formula translation" became a reality. Standards for COBOL and C enabled portability among hardware platforms, and the profession developed

---

2. This section is drawn from *Executable UML: A Foundation for Model-Driven Architecture* by Stephen J. Mellor and Marc J. Balcer (Addison-Wesley, 2002), with permission of the authors. The arguments made there for executable UML rely on raising the level of abstraction as a foundation for model-driven architecture. The same arguments apply here. Reuse in action!

techniques for structuring programs so that they were easier to write, understand, and maintain. We now have languages like Smalltalk, C++, Eiffel, and Java, each with the notion of object-orientation, an approach for structuring data and behavior together into classes and objects.

As we moved from one language to another, generally we increased the level of abstraction at which the developer operates, which required the developer to learn a new, higher-level language that could then be mapped into lower-level ones, from C++ to C to assembly code to machine code and the hardware. At first, each higher layer of abstraction was introduced only as a concept. The first assembly languages were no doubt invented without the benefit of an (automated) assembler to turn mnemonics into bits, and developers were grouping functions together with the data they encapsulated long before there was any automatic enforcement of the concept. Similarly, the concepts of structured programming were taught before there were structured programming languages in widespread industrial use (for instance, Pascal).

Over time, however, the new layers of abstraction became formalized, and tools such as assemblers, preprocessors, and compilers were constructed to support the concepts. This had the effect of hiding the details of the lower layers so that only a few experts (compiler writers, for example) needed to concern themselves with the details of how those layers work. In turn, this raises concerns about the loss of control induced by, for example, eliminating the GOTO statement or writing in a high-level language at a distance from the "real machine." Indeed, sometimes the next level of abstraction has been too big a reach for the profession as a whole, only of interest to academics and purists, and the concepts did not take a large enough mindshare to survive. (ALGOL-68 springs to mind. So does Eiffel, but it has too many living supporters to be a safe choice of example.)

As the profession has raised the level of abstraction at which developers work, we have developed tools to map from one layer to the next automatically. Developers now write in a high-level language that can be mapped to a lower-level language automatically, instead of writing in the lower-level language that can be mapped to assembly language, just as our predecessors wrote in assembly language and had that translated automatically into machine language.

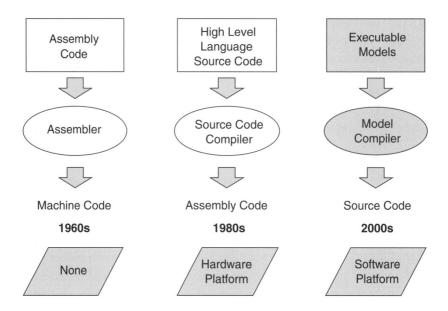

Figure 1-1 Raising the level of abstraction

Clearly, this forms a pattern: We formalize our knowledge of an application in as high a level a language as we can. Over time, we learn how to use this language and apply a set of conventions for its use. These conventions become formalized and a higher-level language is born that is mapped automatically into the lower-level language. In turn, this next-higher-level language is perceived as low level, and we develop a set of conventions for its use. These newer conventions are then formalized and mapped into the next level down, and so forth.

The next level of abstraction is the move, shown in Figure 1-1, to model-based development, in which we build software-platform-independent models.

Software-platform independence is analogous to hardware-platform independence. A hardware-platform-independent language, such as C or Java, enables the writing of a specification that can execute on a variety of hardware platforms with no change. Similarly, a software-platform-independent language enables the writing of a specification that can execute on a variety of software platforms, or software architecture designs, with no change. So, a software-platform-independent specification could be mapped to a multiprocessor/multitasking CORBA environment, or a client-server relational database environment, with no change to the model.

In general, the organization of the data and processing implied by a conceptual model may not be the same as the organization of the data and processing in implementation. If we consider two concepts, those of "customer" and "account," modeling them as classes using the UML suggests that the software solution should be expressed in terms of software classes named Customer and Account. However, there are many possible software designs that can meet these requirements, many of which are not even object-oriented. Between concept and implementation, an attribute may become a reference; a class may be divided into sets of object instances according to some sorting criteria; classes may be merged or split; statecharts may be flattened, merged, or separated; and so on. A modeling language that enables such mappings is software-platform independent.

Raising the level of abstraction changes the platform on which each layer of abstractions depends. Model-based development relies on the construction of models that are independent of their software platforms, which include the likes of CORBA, client-server relational database environments, and the very structure of the final code.

Raising the Level of Reuse

Though some pundits have suggested that there has been more reuse of the word "reuse" than practice of it, it's undoubtedly the case that a major area of progress in our industry has involved enabling reuse. In the earliest systems, memory was so expensive that it was often necessary to save memory by reusing inline code. If those ten lines of assembly code were the same for one context as for a second, then the confines of limited memory required their reuse. Of course, over time, the minor distinctions between one context and another required flags to distinguish each case, and reuse in this manner deservedly acquired a poor reputation. The solution to this problem was the invention of the callable function.

Functions, in the mathematical sense of the word, are ideal for encouraging reuse because they transform their inputs into outputs without recourse to any kind of memory, or "state." The square root function, for example, returns the same result for a given input every time. Mathematical functions lend themselves to reusable libraries for just this reason, and they also increase the granularity of reuse.

However, many functions, such as a payroll function, whose output depends on knowledge of previous deductions, employ stored data saved from one invocation to the next. The controlled use of such stored data increased the range of what could be done with reusable functions—more properly, subroutines—and libraries of these subroutines increased mightily in the 1960s and 1970s.

It quickly became apparent that there's value in sharing data between subroutines. The mechanism commonly chosen to implement this concept was a shared (global) data structure. Here swims the fly in this particular ointment: Just as the flags in shared inline code became a maintenance nightmare, so too did shared data structures. When several subroutines each have uncontrolled access to shared data, a change to a data structure in one subroutine leads to the need to change all the other subroutines to match. Thus was born the object.

Objects encapsulate a limited number of subroutines and the data structures on which they operate. By encapsulating data and subroutines into a single unit, the granularity of reuse is increased from the level of a single subroutine, with implicit interfaces over other (unnamed) subroutines, to a group of subroutines with explicit (named) interfaces over a limited group of subroutines. Objects enable reuse on a larger scale.

Objects are still small-scale, though, given the size of the systems we need to build. There is advantage in reusing collections of related objects together. An Account belongs to a Customer, for example; similarly, the object corresponding with a telephone call is conceptually linked to the circuit on which the call is made. In each case, these objects can, and should, be reused together, connected explicitly in the application.

A set of closely related objects, packaged together with a set of defined interfaces, form a component. A component enables reuse at a higher level, because the unit of reuse is larger. However, just as each of the previous stages in increasing granularity raised issues in its usage, so do components. This time, the problem derives from the interfaces. What happens if an interface changes? The answer, of course, is that we have to find each and every place where the interface is used, change it to use the new interface, test that new code, reintegrate, and then retest the system as a whole. A small change in the interface, therefore, leads to many changes in the code.

Dividing work across vertical problem areas and defining interfaces between these areas is also problematic. It's all too typical for a project team to begin with an incomplete understanding of the problem and then divide the work involved in solving the problem amongst several development teams. The teams share defined interfaces, working to build components that can simply be plugged together at the end of the project. Of course, it doesn't usually work that way: Teams can have different understanding of the specifications of each of the components, and even the best-specified interface can be misinterpreted. Components, and their big brothers, frameworks, are rarely plug-and-play, and organizations can spend inordinate amounts of time writing "glue code" to stick components together properly.

The problem is even worse in systems engineering and hardware/software co-design because the teams don't even share a common language or a common development process. The result tends to be a meeting of the two sides in the lab, some months later, with incompatible hardware and software.

Dividing work into horizontal subject-matter areas, or domain models, such as bank, database, authorization, user interface, and so forth, exposes interfaces at the level of rules. "The persistent data of a class is stored as database tables" and "All updates must be authorized" and "Each operation that affects stored data must be confirmed" are all rules that apply uniformly between different domain models. Glue code can be produced automatically based on rules like these. Figure 1-2 illustrates how this progression increases the granularity of reuse.

Design-Time Interoperability

Even with these advances in the level of reuse, we nonetheless have a problem: There's still little reuse of applications.

Over and over, we see systems that are reimplementations of existing functionality built to make use of improved technology, and we see systems that are unable to reuse existing platforms because they've become interwoven with an existing application. Components and frameworks are helping, but there's still significantly more reuse of those closer to the machine. We see more reuse of databases and data servers—general services that rely on implementation technologies—than we see reuse of customer objects, which in turn rely on general services.

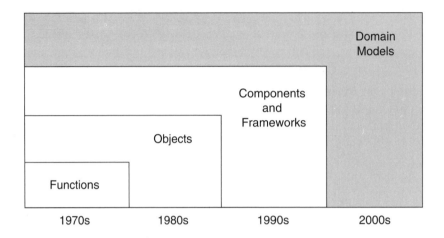

Figure 1-2 Raising the level of reuse

Figure 1-3 shows the overall effect. Each line between layers represents an opportunity for standardization to support run-time interoperability. Standards allow one layer to be replaced by a different implementation that conforms to the same standard. This is the value of interoperability: By defining a standard interface, we may replace one CORBA implementation with another, say, or one SQL database with another.

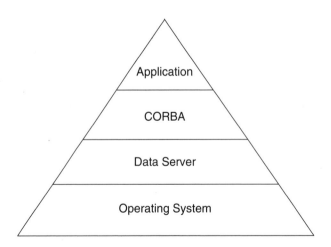

Figure 1-3 The difficulty of reusing applications

Standards and interoperability of this nature certainly help, but the problem still remains: What happens if the CORBA implementation you prefer relies on some operating system or database that you don't want? Tough. You're stuck, because each layer in the pyramid relies on all of the layers below it.

Moreover, components and frameworks may not fit together architecturally. This problem, dubbed *architectural mismatch* by David Garlan (1994), comes about when the several components and/or frameworks in a system have differing concepts about how the system fits together.

Here are some examples, moving from the concrete to the more abstract:

- Two components might each think they have sole control over a resource or device (a printer, for example).
- A component relies on an infrastructure that's completely different from another.
- One component thinks it must request updates, while another thinks it will be told about them.
- One component is event-driven, receiving one set of related data elements at a time, while another periodically updates *all* data elements, whether they're related or not.

In each of these cases, the problem is not merely one of interfaces, though often that's how the problem presents itself, but rather completely different concepts about the software architecture of the system.

Expressed abstractly, reuse at the code level is *multiplicative*, not additive. For example, if there are three possible operating systems, three possible data servers, and three possible CORBA implementations, there are 27 possible implementations ($3 \times 3 \times 3$).

The chances of the stars aligning so we have the right database, the right operating system, and so forth are relatively small (1/27), even though there are only ten components ($3 + 3 + 3$, plus one for the application).

The consequences of this problem are ghastly and gargantuan. Even as we increase the level of abstraction and the level of reuse, we'll continue to have difficulties as the number of layers increases, as it must as we come to tackle ever larger problems. The main reason is that once we've mixed the pieces of code together, it's impossibly difficult to reuse each of the parts, because each part relies so much on code that glues the pieces together—and glue makes everything it touches sticky.

To realize an *additive* solution, one that allows reuse of each layer independently of the others, we must glue layers together using mechanisms that are independent of the content of each layer. These mechanisms are *bridges* between layers, which are expressed as a system of mappings between elements in the layer. Bridges localize the interfaces so that an interface can be changed and subsequently propagated through the code.

Relying on reuse of code, no matter how chunky that code is, addresses only a part of the problem. The dependencies between the layers must be externalized and added in *only when the system is deployed*. The glue must be mixed and applied only at the last moment. Each model is now a reusable, stand-alone asset, not an expense.

Model-driven architecture, then, imposes the system's architecture only at the last moment. In other words, by deferring the gluing of the layers together and combining models at the last (design) minute, model-driven architecture enables *design-time interoperability*.

Models as Assets

Some years ago, one of us was working with a large telecommunications company that was implementing a level-four protocol stack not once, but three times. There were three groups, each in a different part of the U.S., each building essentially the same system. As it turned out, each team was working a slightly different subset on top of different technologies (operating systems, languages, and the like) for different markets. We were able to bring these groups together somewhat, but the reuse we achieved was limited to concepts as expressed informally through the models. Geographical distribution, divergent goals, and just plain politics resulted in three almost completely separate projects.

The cost of building systems this way is enormous. The same system, or a simple subset of it, was implemented with three teams, which tripled the costs. Three times as much code was produced as was required—and that code was then added to the pile o' code the company needed to maintain over time.

In short, software is an expense. And, as we discussed in the previous section, reuse on the application level is often prohibitively difficult. Contrast this situation with the vision promulgated by MDA:

1. Take a model of the protocol stack off the shelf.

2. Subset the model as necessary.

3. Take models of the implementation technologies off the shelf.

4. Describe how the models are to be linked.

5. Generate the system.

When it comes time to change the application, we make the changes in the application model and leave the models of the implementation technologies alone. When we need to retarget an application to a different implementation environment, we select the models for the new environment and regenerate. There's no need to modify the application models. Costs are lower; productivity is higher, based on increased reuse of models; maintenance is cheaper— and each new model that gets built is an asset that can be subsequently reused.

The cost of building and maintaining systems this way is significantly lower. The incremental cost resides primarily in selecting the appropriate models and linking them together. The models themselves need to be constructed, of course, but once they're complete, they have greater longevity than code because they evolve independently of other models. In other words, they become corporate *assets*.

This is *not* just a vision: Systems are being built this way today. But not many systems, unfortunately—most folk are stuck pushing bits in Java or something else. The issue now is to increase the rate of adoption, which we hope will happen as people gain a rich understanding of MDA, starting with Chapter 2.

Chapter 2

MDA Terms and Concepts

There are a lot of acronyms and terms floating around in the world of MDA. This chapter will help you get a grip on the particular meanings of the terms at the heart of MDA, and also provide an overview of what we'll be talking about in the rest of the book.

Models

Models consist of sets of elements that describe some physical, abstract, or hypothetical reality. Good models serve as means of communication; they're cheaper to build than the real thing; and they suit the plan of attack that the team takes toward solving the problem at hand. Models can run the gamut from rough sketches to fairly detailed blueprints to fully executable models; all are useful in the appropriate context.

One key to effective modeling in the context of systems development is good usage of abstraction and classification. **Abstraction** involves ignoring information that is not of interest in a particular context; **classification** involves grouping important information based on common properties, even though the things under study are of course different from one another.

Central to MDA is the notion of creating different models at different levels of abstraction and then linking them together to form an implementation. Some of these models will exist independent of software platforms, while others will be specific to particular platforms. Each model will be expressed using a combination of text and multiple complementary and interrelated diagrams.

The modeling language family of choice today is the UML. The existence of this standard, (reasonably) well-defined language reduces the likelihood of misinterpretation by the viewers of models. In the longer term, defining domain-specific languages (DSLs) using the MDA framework is likely to be an important alternative to the UML.

We look at models in more detail in Chapter 3.

Metamodels and Platforms

A **metamodel** is simply a model of a modelling language. It defines the structure, semantics, and constraints for a family of models. (Note that we're using the term *family* here to group models that share common syntax and semantics.)

A model is captured by a particular metamodel. For example, a model that employs UML diagrams is captured by the UML metamodel, which describes how UML models can be structured, the elements they can contain, and the properties those elements exhibit. In turn, a metamodel may describe some properties of a particular platform, not only the UML, while a platform's properties may be described by more than one metamodel. Figure 2-1 is a UML class diagram that illustrates these relationships.

We define a **platform** as the specification of an execution environment for a set of models. Examples of platforms include the Java platform; CORBA; .NET; operating systems like Linux, Solaris, and Windows; and specific real-time platforms.

Figure 2-1 Models, metamodels, and platforms

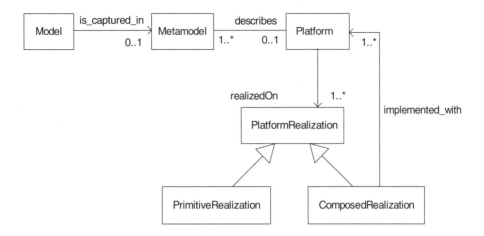

Figure 2-2 Platforms and platform realizations[1]

A platform has to have an implementation of the specification that the platform represents—in other words, at least one realization of it. A realization can in turn build upon one or more other platforms. A realization that stands on its own is a **primitive realization**; a realization comprised of one or more realizations is a **composed realization**. In theory, this *platform stack* can extend down to the level of quantum mechanics, but for our purposes, platforms are only of interest as long as we want to create, edit, or view models that can be executed on them. Figure 2-2 illustrates these concepts in the context of models and metamodels.

The UML metamodel is expressed using the MOF, a facility specified and standardized by the OMG. This metamodel describes many structural and behavioral aspects of UML models, but it doesn't specify how UML models are stored, how they're graphically represented, or how they could be edited by multiple users simultaneously. These are the details that the MOF metamodel abstracts out. What the MOF *does* do is define how models can be accessed and interchanged, in terms of, for example, interfaces defined using the OMG's XML Metadata Interchange (XMI). Other examples of metamodels include the Java language specification and the Common Warehouse Metamodel (CWM).

---

1. Thanks to iO Software for contributing this and other figures that appear in this chapter.

Chapter 4 contains an in-depth exploration of metamodels. Chapter 8 discusses a very important aspect of MDA with regard to a platform stack: linking models within the stack to existing code. Chapter 12 explores platforms in the context of executing an MDA process.

Mapping Between Models

Models may have semantic relationships with other models—for example, when a set of models describes a particular system at different levels of abstraction. As code-driven developers, we construct one model from others by applying a set of implicit rules.

MDA must support iterative and incremental development. This means that mappings between models must be repeatable. This makes it possible to express each aspect of a system at an appropriate level of abstraction while keeping the various models in synch.

Models may have semantic relationships with other models; for example, a set of models may describe a particular system at different levels of abstraction. It's desirable to have mappings between different but related models performed automatically.

A **mapping** between models is assumed to take one or more models as its input (these are the "sources") and produce one output model (this is the "target"). The rules for the mapping are described by **mapping rules** within a **mapping function**; the mapping is an application of the mapping function. These rules are described at the metamodel level in such a way that they're applicable to all sets of source models that conform to the given metamodel.

Figure 2-3 extends Figure 2-1 with illustrations of these concepts.

A person involved in an MDA-compatible process can automate a mapping function by providing an executable specification of it. Such an implementation allows for the automation of important steps of an MDA-driven process. However, this implementation isn't required as long as one can verify any manually conducted mapping against the specification that the mapping function provides.

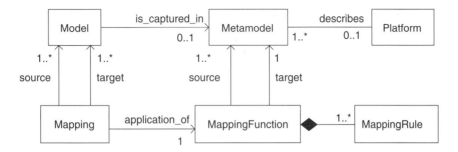

Figure 2-3 Mappings, mapping functions, and mapping rules

For example, a mapping function that describes how to map a UML model of an application to a corresponding Java source code model may be "A UML class maps to a Java class declaration, where the name of the Java class matches the name of the UML class." The transformation can be performed, albeit expensively, by hand, and checked for correctness.

We take a closer look at mappings and mapping functions in Chapter 5.

Marking Models

A mapping rule that, for example, turns a UML attribute into transient data on the heap may not always be appropriate. In some cases, there may also be a need for persistent attributes, so we need to have two mapping rules and additional mapping inputs that select which rule to apply. These additional mapping inputs take the form of **marks,** which are lightweight, nonintrusive extensions to models that capture information required for model transformation without polluting those models.

A mapping may use several different marks associated with the source models; conversely, a mark may cater to several different mappings. There also may be global marks that aren't necessarily related to individual model elements. However, marks mustn't be *integrated* into the source model, because they are specific to the *mapping*, and several different mapping rules may exist, each of which requires different marks. Integrating the marks with the model would make the model specific to the corresponding mapping rules, which isn't desirable. You can think of marks as a set of "sticky notes," attached to the elements of a source model, that direct the model transformer.

You can use marks in two contexts: as additional *inputs*, which you can use to anticipate design decisions or reuse design decisions across mapping functions, and as additional *outputs*, which serve as a kind of record of the transformation process from a source model to a target model.

A mark is defined by a **marking model**, which describes the structure and semantics of a set of types of marks. A mapping function specifies the marking models whose types of marks it requires on the instances of its source metamodels.

If a mapping function can use more than one marking model for a single source metamodel, then one can reuse marking models for several different mapping functions. This, in turn, renders the corresponding marks reusable for different corresponding mappings. Figure 2-4 illustrates these concepts.

Figure 2-5 illustrates the idea that marking a model for different mappings leads to different **platform-specific models (PSMs)**.

The source model for these mappings is a **platform-independent model (PIM)** with regard to the target platforms *A* and *B*. The marks don't pollute the PIM, which allows the PIM to be mapped repeatedly to two different PSMs.

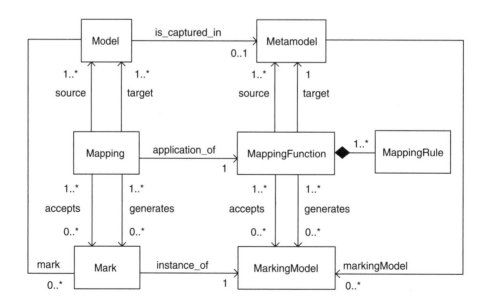

Figure 2-4 Marks and marking models

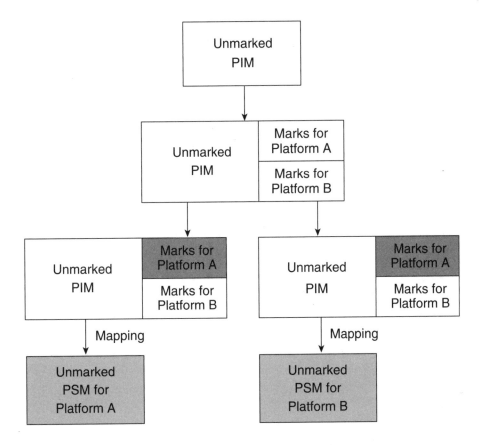

Figure 2-5 From PIMs to PSMs

We explore PIMs and PSMs further in Chapter 4. Marks and marking models are discussed in detail in Chapter 6.

Building Languages

In the normal course of development, people build languages on a regular basis. For instance, when they use a subset of the UML for *analysis* and a larger subset for *design*, and when they specify what the elements of these subsets actually mean, they've defined two new languages, each with a different purpose.

There are two major reasons to seek relatively formal definitions of new languages in the context of MDA. The first is communication among team members. There needs to be agreement on whether to include things like persistence, and many other issues like it, in a certain model, and on how to represent those things. The second is communication with machines. Defining languages formally allows for mappings between models expressed in those languages.

One way to define a language involves using the MOF, which supports several important concepts that can serve as the foundation for a new language. Since the metamodel for the UML is already defined using these core concepts, it's relatively straightforward to use the MOF to define a language this way. Another way involves extending the UML via **profiles**, which are mechanisms for adapting an existing metamodel with constructs that are specific to a particular domain, platform, or method. The key elements of profiles are **stereotypes**, which extend the basic vocabulary of the UML, and **constraints**, which specify conditions within a model that must hold true for the model to be "well-formed."

Note that the "definition" of a language is, strictly speaking, the **abstract syntax**, which addresses the structure of the language separated from its concrete notational symbols. Defining a graphical notation for a new language—in other words, a *concrete* syntax and notation to use in creating, editing, and maintaining the models expressed in that language—is a separate problem. Fortunately, there are straightforward ways to represent a new language graphically using the MOF and the UML; these include mapping functions and marks in addition to models and the underlying metamodel.

Chapter 7 explores the topic of building languages in some depth.

Model Elaboration

Model elaboration is the idea that a model can be modified after it has been generated. Usually, this means adding code to the model, but it can also mean editing the generated model itself. This possibility of elaboration of target models is an advantage of the MDA framework because it allows developers to ease into model-driven development, rather than take a step function from a code-driven process to a model-driven one.

To get the most out of model elaboration, it's important to follow certain principles:

- Don't elaborate a model if you don't have to.
- Don't elaborate "intermediate" models that aren't meant to be exposed.
- Localize elaboration and avoid redundancy in elaborating locations.

If it's done carefully, then, elaborating models can be a perfectly acceptable practice in the context of MDA.

When the target model is regenerated, one needs to be certain that this added code isn't replaced by the regenerated code. A simple approach is the concept of protected areas: If an area of the source model is protected, the mapping function can try to preserve the manually-entered contents. Detecting manual changes in target models, preserving/merging manual changes during mapping, and avoiding the loss of manually-created information are critical success factors in this area.

The reverse engineering of models, and their bidirectional synchronization, is also of interest in this context. One-time usage of an **abstracting mapping**, which pulls the contents of a detailed model into a more abstract model for subsequent mapping to other more detailed models, can be very useful.

We explore these topics further in Chapter 8.

Executable Models

The next logical step is to **executable models**, which have everything required to produce the desired functionality of a single domain. These models are neither sketches nor blueprints; as their name suggests, models run. This allows us to deliver a running system in small increments in direct communication with customers.

Executable models act just like code, in a sense, though they also provide the ability to interact directly with the customer's domain, which is something code doesn't do well. They're not exactly the same as code, though, because they need to be woven together with other models (for example, a meaningful user interface) to produce a system. This is generally done by a **model compiler**. As each model is complete in itself, though, once the weaving is done, the system is complete.

Just as programming languages conferred independence from the hardware platform, executable models confer independence from the software platform, which makes executable models portable across multiple development environments. Contrast this with adding code bodies to models. Such code bodies are inherently dependent on the structure of the platform for which the code is intended.

One way to express executable models involves the use of **Executable UML,** a profile of the UML that defines an execution semantics for a carefully selected, streamlined subset of the UML. The subset is computationally complete, so an executable UML model can be directly executed. Executable UML defines groupings of data and behavior ("classes"), the behavior over time of instances ("state charts"), and precise computational behavior ("actions") *without* prescribing implementation.

Chapter 9 offers details about executable models and Executable UML.

Agile MDA

Agile MDA is based on the notion that code and executable models are operationally the same. It employs executable models so they may be immediately tested and verified by running them, which provides for immediate feedback to customers and domain experts from running models.

Agile MDA addresses the potential conflict between MDA and agile methods, which propose to address the problems associated with the "verification gap" (which comes about when one writes documents that can't be executed) by delivering small slices of working code as soon as possible. This working functionality is immediately useful to the customer, who can interact with it; this might result in improved understanding on the customer's part of the system that needs to be built. As these delivery cycles can be short (say, a week or two), the system's development process is able to adapt to changing conditions and deliver just what the customer wants.

Each model necessarily conforms to the same metamodel, because all models are equal—there are no "analysis" or "design" models. Models are linked together, rather than transformed, and all of them are then mapped to a single combined model that is subsequently translated into code according to a single system architecture.

We expand the discussion of agile MDA in Chapter 10.

Building an MDA Process

After all of the discussion of the various aspects of MDA, at some point, one needs a process. We started this chapter by talking about models, which of course are at the heart of MDA. At the heart of defining an MDA process, by extension, is the identification of these models.

Think of the gap that separates a problem statement from a coded system. If the gap is narrow enough, you can simply hop across, but if it's wider, you need some stepping stones. The stones represent the models you select; each step from one stone to another represents a mapping function. The path from one side to the other constitutes a particular **mapping chain** for this project.

Deciding where to place the stones, and planning the journey from one side to the other, constitutes a definition for an **MDA process**. The selection of the models and the mapping functions between them must fit together to form the specific process you apply on your MDA project.

The best approach to building an MDA process involves a combination of two approaches: (1) focusing on finding models that exist at a single level of abstraction, and (2) focusing on the length of the mapping chain and finding an optimal length for each "hop" in the chain. A multiple-hop approach tends to simplify the mapping functions; it exposes an intermediate model (which sits between the source model and the target model) so the mapping functions can be reused. The choice of intermediate domains may also depend on what is available for reuse (possibly from third parties).

An effective approach is to divide up the system into independent subject matters, or **problem domains**. These subject matters can be displayed on a **domain chart**, which shows the domains and the bridges—in other words, the mapping functions, marks, and marking models—between them. The domain chart forms the basis for defining the MDA process for your project.

Chapter 11 provides more detail about defining an MDA process.

Executing an MDA Process

Once one has an MDA process in place, one naturally wants to execute it. Broadly speaking, this comes down to two main activities: (1) formalizing knowledge of a subject matter and then rendering that knowledge as an implementation, and (2) mapping that formalized knowledge onto a target platform that can execute.

Knowledge formalization, in the context of MDA, involves, as you might expect, gathering requirements relevant to the domain of interest, abstracting that knowledge into some set of concepts, and then expressing those concepts formally in a model. What MDA brings to the table is the concept of testing the model for correctness—preferably by executing it.

As the models start coming together, the next step is to build bridges among them. This involves specifying and verifying mapping functions, building marking models, and then transforming the models. Once the models are marked and the mapping function specifications are complete, one can transform the formalized, marked, and verified knowledge into other models or source code comprising the system's implementation.

Further exploration of how to execute an MDA process, along with an example process based on the banking system example, is provided in Chapter 12.

Chapter 3

Building Models

Chapter 1 and Chapter 2 outlined the rationale for MDA and the main technical areas. Now it's time to explore these in more depth and show how it all works. We start with the *sine qua non*, the most important of them all, models.

Why Model?

Software is getting easier to develop, thanks to the best efforts of computer language inventors, tool developers, and process gurus, but the process of getting from a set of requirements to a proper abstraction of the solution remains difficult. Even relatively small systems can have large amounts of complexity, which is what leads people to develop models. A **model** is a simplification of something so we can view, manipulate, and reason about it, and so help us understand the complexity inherent in the subject under study.

A wide variety of models have been in use within various engineering disciplines for a long time. Aerospace engineers rely heavily on models that describe the forces acting on an airplane; electrical engineers use large models to design telephone switching systems; civil engineers would be lost without their blueprints. Other forms of models, such as the simulations used in high finance and the storyboarding that Hollywood directors use, also play important roles.

We can say the following things about what makes a good model:

- A good model omits information in order to help viewers more clearly see the issue at hand and check the correctness of the developed understanding. A good model will therefore *not* be the same as the real thing in all respects. For example, we may model an airplane to understand how well it will fly by omitting details about interior fittings.

- A good model accurately reflects some real, abstract, or hypothetical reality. That is, although the model omits information, the information that remains accurately captures the subject matter at hand so we can reason about it. For example, the lack of interior fittings is generally unimportant in understanding aerodynamic behavior, yet the weight distribution of those same fittings can affect aerodynamics.

- A good model must be cheaper to build than the real thing. Note that we don't mean cheaper only in the financial sense. We might build models of medical instruments or spacecraft so we can experiment with the models or use them to verify correct behavior before building the real thing, because the real thing comes with risks with regard to human life.

- A good model serves as a means of communication by illustrating one or more ideas quickly and easily. A standard, well-defined modeling language reduces the likelihood of misinterpretation by the viewers of the model, including machines. MDA takes advantage of that fact to provide automation to we the cobblers' children.

Abstraction, Classification, and Generalization

No matter the discipline, a modeler ignores some information that is not of interest and groups important information together based on common properties, even though the entities under study are, of course, different from one another. This is where abstraction and classification come into play.

"Abstracts" is the ideologically sound term for just ignoring something (it sounds like a whole lot more work), while "classifies" captures the notion of grouping based on common properties. Both take place in many contexts, but one crucial area is the formalization of knowledge of some universe of discourse in a model.

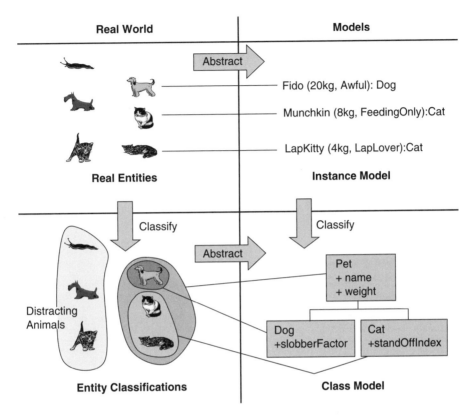

Figure 3-1 Abstraction, classification, and generalization

Suppose, for example, we're faced with a pet store whose owner needs some software to help in the business. Figure 3-1 shows the relationship between the animals and the concepts of abstraction and classification.

Broadly speaking, abstraction involves moving from the left column to the right one, while classification involves moving from the upper row to the lower one. Allow us to explain.

The upper left-hand corner shows a universe of discourse that contains various real, abstract, or hypothetical things, in this case, a cat Munchkin, a dog Fido, and an unnamed slug (it's not a pet, so why would it have a name?). We classify these creatures according to their common properties: All dogs slobber to a certain degree, and all cats are more or less standoffish or cuddly.

These groupings, Dogs, Cats, and Distracting Animals, are shown in the lower left-hand corner.

Note that classifying things does *not* change the amount of detail; rather, it is more a grouping or set-building operation that finds commonalities and arranges common instances into the same class.

The second important dimension is that of abstraction. Some properties of a pet are not relevant, such as the precise color of its fur or its sleeping habits. Some of the creatures we find aren't themselves relevant—they exist, but their primary property of interest is that we don't care much. We abstract away from each entity's original properties, leaving only those of interest. Note that abstraction *doesn't* mean that the real-world pet's peculiarities that its owner love have gone away; rather, abstraction collars only the properties of interest.

Common features of both dogs and cats (in this case, name and weight) have also been generalized into a separate class, Pet. This grouping of common features of all pets is called **generalization**. It is "double-strength" classification, in that a single beast, say Fido, has been classified both as a Dog and as a Pet.

A modeler typically combines the three steps of classifying, abstracting, and generalizing, and thus accomplishes them simultaneously. That is, he or she looks at the problem domain—the real Fido, Fifi, Munchkin, and Squishy (even a slug has a name to his mates)—and abstracts away unwanted information at the same time that he or she classifies the problem-domain things into types. We just know that both Rex and Fido are dogs, and that cats and dogs are pets. In our heads, we classify all of these pets that the store has (or will ever have) in stock, each of which has its own name and weight and so forth, into a few entities: the Pet class, with subclasses for Dog, Cat, and so forth. At the same time, we start to think about the properties of these classes, which we previously abstracted away during generalization, and attribute these properties to the right groups. So, we've abstracted, classified, and generalized the set of animals in what seemed to be a single step.

The right-hand column of Figure 3-1 represents the modeling realm. The class diagram at the bottom captures the types and their properties of interest, as well as the generalization relationships that we identified during the classification step. The upper right-hand quadrant represents the objects in our system, each of which is an instance of a particular class in the modeling realm.

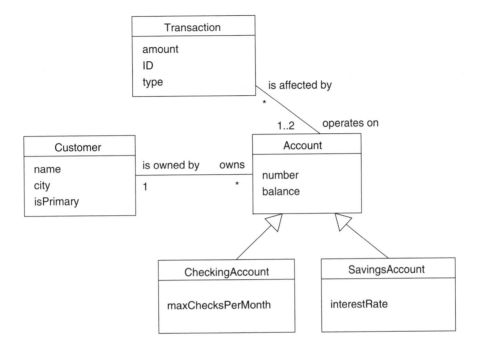

Figure 3-2 Domain-level class diagram for banking model

The instances we've created are abstractions of the original problem-domain things, but only with the properties of interest. Hence, the object referred to by pointer F1D0 is the abstracted computer version of the real-world Fido. (Cloning aside, we can't magically instantiate real-world cats and dogs.)

Subject Matter and Language Abstraction

Figure 3-2 shows some of the conceptual entities associated with a banking system, which we have abstracted, classified, and generalized by examining "real" customers, accounts, and transactions and capturing their critical properties, such as customer city, account balance, and transaction amount. In so doing, our modeler has abstracted away irrelevant properties, such as a customer's salary, number of children, and ghastly personal habits. However, the model also has abstracted away information that's required to make the system work properly, such as how we know that Fred (an object of class Customer) truly is Fred when he attempts to withdraw money from his account.

This security information has been abstracted away because it belongs to a different subject matter, or problem domain. The bank can be modeled without reference to security, so long as—somehow—we can establish that a customer really is who he or she claims to be. Obversely, the problem of identifying and authenticating a person, and authorizing his or her operations, occurs in many systems, not just banking, and security can be modeled without reference to banking, as it would have to be in a building security or network security problem, say. We can then model the bank without worrying about security at all, and model security without worrying about its potential applications. It is then a separate problem to hook the two models together to create an implementation, and so specify where security applies within the banking model.

This, of course, is exactly what MDA does.

Ignoring whole subject matters is a form of abstraction. The banking model ignored security, and the security model ignored other subject matters, so that each model can stand alone, as a separate problem domain.

A **problem domain** is a subject matter that can be understood independently of other subject matters. A problem domain can be based around some "real" world, such as customers and accounts for a bank, or it can be less concrete, such as a model of security, or even an operating system.

Figure 3-3 shows an excerpt from a typical Security model that our banking system might use. This is a typical set of classes for role-based access control.

The classes on this diagram are:

- A *ProtectedResource* is something affected by system actions.
- A *ProtectedAction* is an action that is subject to authorization.
- A *Principal* is a human being or application operating as an authorized user of a system on whose behalf actions are triggered.
- A *Role* defines a relationship between a Principal and the system.
- A *Permission* reflects the actions that a Principal, acting in a particular Role, can take with regard to a particular ProtectedResource.

Separately, each domain model is expressed in some kind of modeling language. Mathematical equations are one language that we may use to describe air flow over a wing; symbols for resistors, capacitors, and various integrated circuits constitute a language used by electrical engineers; scale drawings help civil engineers; and Hollywood gets by on recreational drugs.

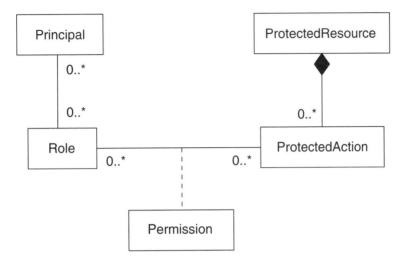

Figure 3-3 Domain-level class diagram for security domain

Any modeling language allows you to say some things but not others. For example, an association between Customers and Accounts captures the notion that customers own their related accounts, but it doesn't say whether to use a linked list, pointers, or hash tables. This comes about because the language itself exists at a particular level of abstraction.

By thinking about the problem at a high level of abstraction, specifying a system is much more convenient, efficient, and reusable. We increase productivity because we can say more, more quickly. The higher the level of the language, the greater the amount of functionality that can be delivered for a given amount of effort.

In addition, we can perform a transformation from one level of language abstraction to another. For example, we could decide that every association will be implemented by a pointer. In other words, a large amount of detail in one language can automatically be derived from an abstract specification in another language.

Often, these two kinds of abstraction—ignoring subject matters and ignoring realizations—are conflated. When we elaborate our banking model to include behavior related to security, and various implementation technologies as well, we change the level of subject-matter abstraction and language abstraction at the same time.

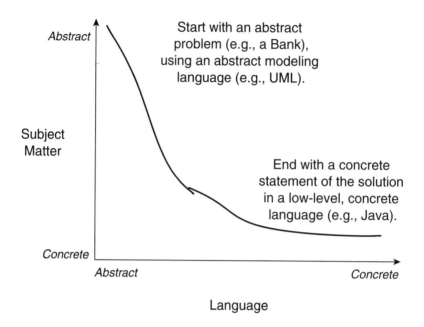

Figure 3-4 Subject matter and modeling language abstraction levels

Figure 3-4 illustrates this situation. Both axes denote an abstraction level, one for the subject matter and the other for the modeling language. Note that the axis marked Language is inverted so that a high level of abstraction is near the origin. This allows us to draw the curve from the upper left to the lower right that shows decreasing abstraction in the subject matter at the same time as decreasing abstraction in the modeling language. In short, as we progress from, say, analysis to design, the subject matter and the modeling language both become less abstract.

Of course, it doesn't have to be this way. There's nothing to prevent one from specifying the behavior of the bank in Java or Smalltalk, and indeed some folks, in particular those in the Extreme Programming (XP) camp, promote exactly this idea. It's also perfectly reasonable to express a model of an implementation technology in a highly abstract analysis language, such as the UML, which one might want to do in the context of merging models, which we discuss in Chapter 6.

Model Projections

For a model to be useful, we not only need to be able to abstract away presently-not-relevant subject matters, and use a language at an appropriate level of abstraction, but we should also try not to show everything at once. For example, combining a class diagram with communication diagrams to show both static structure and the dynamic behavior of customers and their accounts would quickly become too confusing for a viewer of the diagrams to understand. Consequently, we need multiple complementary and interrelated projections that, when taken together, form a complete model. (Note that we're using "projection" to mean a representation of some sort, and "model" to mean the underlying set of abstractions, classifications, behaviors, and so forth. In this manner, each diagram is a representation of some projection on a model.)

It's not unreasonable to treat subsets of models (or single diagrams, for that matter) as models in their own right, and to use mapping functions to map between them, as one might if one were to, for example, populate a communication diagram from function invocations and signal-sending actions on a statechart diagram. However, it simplifies the discussion to treat this as a special case, where the level of abstraction of the languages used in the two diagrams is the same.

This brings us to yet another form of abstraction: simply leaving stuff out. Some models may be plain incomplete at a given level of language abstraction. MDA is perfectly happy with this situation in general (so long as the missing elements are added eventually, of course). A typical situation where this occurs is in the addition of handcrafted code. There's nothing wrong in having MDA support handcrafted code, as long as you don't take it as an "out" but instead use it with care. As a rule, you should express everything you can in the model. We discuss how you should approach adding and maintaining handcrafted code to a model in Chapter 8.

Models and Platforms

The discussion so far has concerned itself with the various properties of a single model. However, MDA is all about transforming between models, each of which captures one or more subject matters and each of which is expressed in a language with a specific degree of abstraction.

Platform independence is a relative concept. One way to look at it is to refer to the curve in Figure 3-4. For two arbitrary models, the one that's higher up the curve is more platform-independent, while the one lower down is more platform-specific. It's the smoothness of this curve, and the mixing of subject matters, that is the genesis of the endless arguments about what constitutes *analysis* and what constitutes *design*. It's also at the heart of continuing discussions today about what constitutes platform independence.

The politically correct way of thinking about this is to define two kinds of models, as described below.

A **PIM** is a model of a subject matter, such as banking, telephony, or the operation of a copier. A PIM's metamodel (see Metamodels and Platforms in Chapter 2) represents abstractions from one or more platform models. For example, a PIM of a bank need not capture the details of security, a network, or a persistence mechanism.

A **PSM**, as the name suggests, is a model that relies on details about platforms. A PSM of a bank-with-database, for example, would refer to tables for persistent data describing accounts and also classes for transient information about those accounts. (In this sense, the bank and the database are combined, though the database software has a life of its own.) As another example, certain banking operations may be combined with other operations that check the identity of the requestor, thereby providing for "security level 3," whatever that might be. In this case, a PSM is more clearly a weaving together of the elements of the PIM and of the required platforms, a database, and a security mechanism.

Figure 3-2 showed a portion of a PIM that represents a typical bank. This model didn't reference distributed objects and remote accessibility, even though we happen to know that the design will use a target technology that offers both locally and remotely accessible objects.

We've chosen to abstract away this technology in the analysis model for the usual reasons: The operation of remote objects is not of interest with regard to the subject matter of the bank, and this additional information unnecessarily clutters the model and the business expert's mind. As a consequence, we've chosen to use an analysis modeling language at a level of abstraction that can't describe remote accessibility.

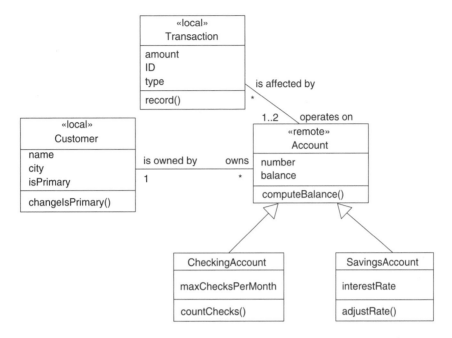

Figure 3-5 Design-level class diagram for banking model

Figure 3-5 shows a PSM for the bank with references to platform-specific concepts, namely access to remote and local objects. The PSM refers to additional information about the implementation. (Note the UML stereotypes on the Customer, Transaction, and Account classes, which specify which classes are "local" and which are "remote.")

The PSM uses a modeling language at a lower level of abstraction than the analysis model; it includes classes and other model elements that capture how, in this example, to effect remote accessibility. In other words, the design model has changed both the level of abstraction of the modeling language and the subject matter, in this case by conjoining banking stuff with technology stuff.

Using Models

We build models to increase productivity, under the justified assumption that it's cheaper to manipulate the model than the real thing. Models then enable cheaper exploration and reasoning about some universe of discourse. One important application of models is to understand a real, abstract, or hypothetical problem domain that a computer system will reflect. This is done by abstraction, classification, and generalization of subject-matter entities into an appropriate set of classes and their behavior.

The subject matter may be far away from the implementation, such as the bank under study, or it may be relatively close to the implementation, such as a database. Similarly, the language we use to express the model may exhibit a high degree of abstraction or it may be a low-level language. The UML may serve as the modeling language in all of these cases, though we generally use some subset of it.

In the bad old days before MDA, these models served only to facilitate communication between customers and developers and act as blueprints for construction. Nowadays, MDA establishes the infrastructure for defining and executing transformations between models of various kinds.

MDA *per se* is relaxed about exactly what models it transforms, so long as the modeling language in which the models are expressed can be defined. How to do that is the topic of the next chapter.

Chapter 4

Building Metamodels

The Greek prefix "meta-" means *after* or *beyond*. It's time now to move beyond the simple construction of models into the construction of models of models—or, more accurately, models of modeling languages.

Why Metamodels?

So, what's the point of having metamodels, and why should you care? Because models must be stated in a way that yields a common understanding among all involved parties, we need a way to specify exactly what a model means. Metamodels allow you to do just that: They specify the concepts of the language you're using to specify a model.

Metamodels simplify communication *about* models. Rather than say "A Customer is something that can have attributes and operations and whose instances potentially live as long as the software system lives," we can simply say "Customer is an instance of Entity," or even just "the Customer entity," and refer to the appropriate metamodel that tells us precisely what an Entity is (something that can have attributes and operations and whose instances potentially live as long as the software system lives, presumably).

Moreover, mapping functions (see Mapping Between Models in Chapter 2) can be stated crisply using concepts defined in the metamodel. For example, a mapping function could state that an element of the source model, such as

Class, corresponds with an element of the target model, such as Entity. The key ideas here are that the meaning of *class* is defined in a metamodel and that the meaning of *entity* is also defined in a (different) metamodel.

These three reasons—specification of the language, communication about models, and a way to specify mapping functions—constitute compelling reasons to venture into The Meta-Zone.

Metamodels

A metamodel is the result of a process of abstraction, classification, and generalization on the problem domain of the modeling language. The box that we commonly think of as a *class* is a concept in a modeling language, as are the other concepts we know from the UML, such as operations, activities, and states. Fundamentally, then, a **metamodel** is a model of the modeling language.

Figure 4-1 shows a small subset of the UML metamodel. ("Small" actually doesn't do it justice. There are 805 pages of text in the recently released UML 2.0 specification [Object Management Group, 2003], supported by goodness knows how many figures.) The classes in the metamodel capture the concepts Class, Property, Operation, and so forth that we use to build UML models. The metamodel also says that a Class is a subclass of Classifier, and a Class can have many Properties. The metamodel, then, formalizes our knowledge about what the UML *is*.

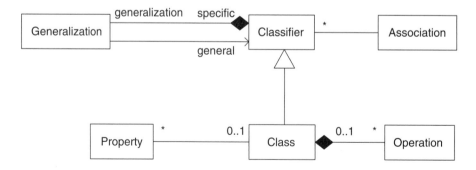

Figure 4-1 Excerpt from the UML metamodel

Note that we're using the UML as an example. We could build a model of any arbitrary modeling language, and all of the same arguments would apply. We chose the UML as an example because, as the introduction to every UML-related academic paper since 1998 will tell you, it is the *lingua franca* of systems development.

Figure 4-2 shows the relationship between the metamodel and the pet model we introduced in Chapter 3.

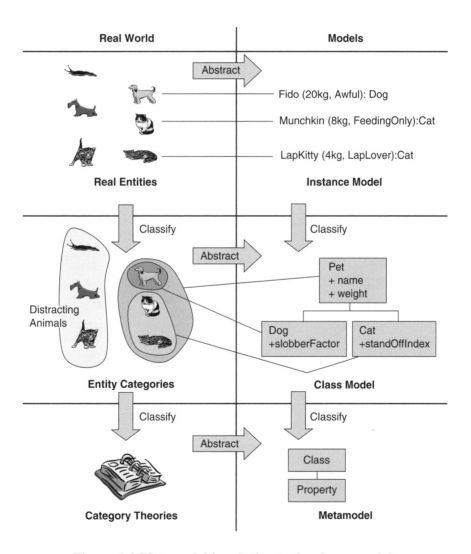

Figure 4-2 Metamodel in relation to developer models

This sketch extends Figure 3-1 to show the relationship of the metamodel to the model. Whereas the types defined for the problem domain under study were Pet, Cat, and Dog, now that we shift down one level, the problem domain under study is the modeling language itself. The types in the language are Class, Property, Operation, Generalization, and so on—the classes that appear in Figure 4-1.

The third row in Figure 4-2 represents the model beyond the model—in other words, the metamodel. The metamodel is a model of the modeling language: a model of the UML.

Now, this is where it gets weird.

The instances of the class Class have values that are themselves classes from the original developer's model. This relationship is often informally called the *instance-of* relationship. The two best-known examples of the instance-of relationship are an object being an instance of a class and a row in a relational database being an instance of a table definition.

It's important to recognize that this instance-of relationship—the one that is "meta"—is different from the instance-of relationship that relates instances at the same level, such as that between Fido and the object pointed to by F1D0. This distinction is drawn out in (Atkinson and Kuhne).

Figure 4-3 shows how the excerpt from the analysis model of our banking system relates to the UML metamodel, which is represented by Multiplicity, Association, Class, and Generalization. We could perform the same exercise for the design model we introduced in Chapter 3. A metamodel, then, has types from another model as its instances.

When you're using your UML tool, you draw a rectangular class shape to denote a model element that has properties. That act creates an instance of the class Class with the name of the class you specify, and instances of the class Property that also have names that you specify. Similarly, when you use a line to connect class shapes, the line expresses the fact that there is an Association between one Class and another. (Your tool also captured other information, such as the location of the boxes on the screen, so that the model can be redrawn at a later date, but that doesn't concern us here.)

What you've done, in fact, is to use the UML modeling language to capture your model implicitly in the UML's (explicit) metamodel.

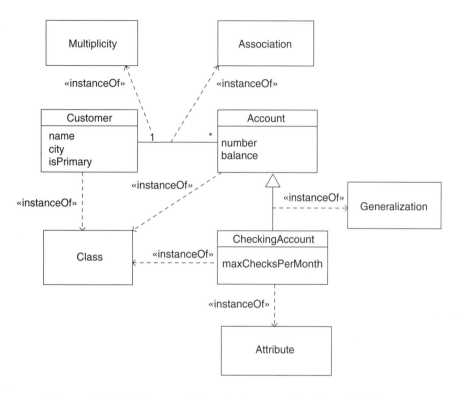

Figure 4-3 Banking model as instances of metamodel classes

The Four-Layer Architecture

The three layers of Figure 4-2, which comprise objects, models, and meta-models, are universal, and the OMG has standardized a terminology to ease communication about them, as shown in Figure 4-4.

- **M0** contains the data of the application (for example, the instances populating an object-oriented system at runtime, or rows in relational database tables). (This is the top row in Figure 4-2.)

- **M1** contains the application: the classes of an object-oriented system, or the table definitions of a relational database. This is the level at which application modeling takes place (the type or model level). (This is the second row in Figure 4-2.)

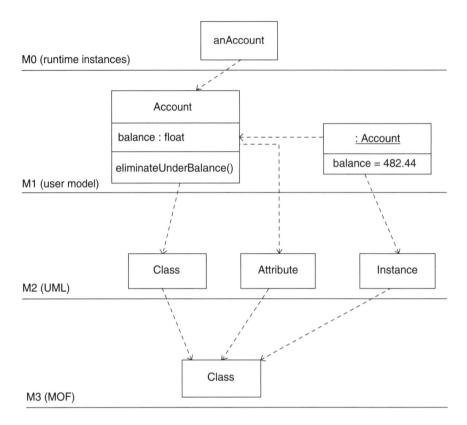

Figure 4-4 Four-level metamodel hierarchy

- **M2** contains the metadata that captures the modeling language: UML elements such as Class, Attribute, and Operation. This is the level at which tools operate (the metamodel or architectural level). (This is the bottom row in Figure 4-2.)

In each case above, the M stands for "meta," unsurprisingly. As we mentioned before, the levels are relative.

There can also be models that span more than one of these levels, such as a UML model that describes both the data and the metadata of an application by means of object diagrams and class diagrams, respectively. Note the Account class and its instance depicted at the same M-level in Figure 4-4.

Despite its prominence, the UML metamodel is just another metamodel. There were many notations available in the dark days before UML, and each of them could have been (and some were) metamodeled. This fact raises the question of whether it is possible to build a metamodel of the metamodel, and the answer is Yes:

- **M3** is the metametadata that describes the properties that metadata can exhibit. This is the level at which modeling languages and metamodels operate, providing for interchange between tools.

  The fundamental idea behind this level in the hierarchy is that there are classes whose instances can be associated with instances of other classes, have attributes of some type, and perform operations. In other words, M3 describes the modeling paradigm.

  In turn, it's reasonable to ask if it's possible to build a metameta-metamodel. (Really!) The answer is both Yes and No. Yes, we could build a metamodel of M3, but the modeling language we use would itself be at M3. If there were an M4, it would look just the same as M3. So, there is nothing beyond M3, because M3 is self-describing.

  Assigning fixed numbers to the levels can be misleading at times. It's more useful to regard the relationships among the four levels—in other words, the metarelations—as relative. Some x can be "meta" to some y if x says something about y. At the same time, y can be "meta" to some z in the same way, and so forth. Everything is relative.

  Nonetheless, the M3 level is a model of only the simplest set of concepts required to capture models and metamodels. M3 stands out as a constant in the modeling business. That's why there have been some efforts in standardizing things at this level, which has given us the MOF.

MOF: A Standard For Metamodeling

The **MOF** defines a set of modeling constructs that a modeler can use to define and manipulate a set of interoperable metamodels. The MOF resides at the bottom (M3) level of the four-tier metamodel architecture. It captures the structure and semantics of arbitrary metamodels—in particular, the UML metamodel—and also various kinds of metadata.

Interoperability of metamodels across domains is required for integrating tools and applications across a development lifecycle using common semantics. In addition to being a metamodeling tool, the MOF also provides for standard data access, by defining supporting standards to be used by MOF-compliant languages to exchange and access complying models. One application of this, as we shall see next, involves applying mapping functions to models.

One of these supporting standards is **XMI**, which defines rules for deriving an XML schema from a MOF-compliant modeling language as well as rules for rendering a compliant model into a compliant XML document. The combination of MOF and standards such as XMI serves as the backbone of a basic MDA infrastructure that enables us to talk of a more sophisticated infrastructure featuring the likes of marking models and mapping functions, and eventually an MDA superstructure that features custom metamodels and profiles.

The UML is more comprehensive than the MOF, with its support for use cases and elaborate behavioral modeling, its graphical notation, and its extensibility mechanisms. The OMG has striven for a unification of the MOF and UML cores. This will make the UML's graphical notation usable also for MOF metamodels. Note that this doesn't mean there is a graphical notation for the metamodels *defined* with MOF. Chapter 7 describes how you can use the UML to find graphical notations for your own metamodels defined in MOF.

Using Metamodels

We build (or use preexisting) metamodels to declare the elements of a modeling language so we can build mappings between them. (There are other uses, such as building a language, which we take up in Chapter 7.)

A metamodel is merely a model whose instances are types in another model. This allows us to capture the *other* model and manipulate it. A well-known metamodel is the specification for UML, which captures the classes in a developer's model. Moreover, metamodels may themselves be captured in metametamodels, the OMG standard form for which is the MOF. The MOF provides the means by which you will be able to tailor your metamodels and relate them to a standard MDA infrastructure. The existence of standards for representing models, metamodels, and metametamodels forms the backbone of the MDA infrastructure.

A primary application for metamodels is to enable the definition of transformations between models. To build such transformations, you have to understand the modeling language in which the source and the target models are expressed—which is to say, the source and target models as prescribed by the metamodels. We take up this topic in more detail in Chapter 5.

Chapter 5

Building Mappings

...apter describes the whys and wherefores of mapping between models. ...ssic example is a mapping from an *analysis* model to a *design* model. ...shall see, this is just one of many possible kinds of mapping.

...ping is defined by a mapping function, which is comprised of mapping ...When a mapping is executed between a source model and a target ...it defines some or all of the content of the target model.

...atic model transformations increase portability and development effi-..., which in turn increases software quality while lowering development time and cost. MDA incorporates automatic transformations into the early stages of software development.

Why Mappings?

Consider a platform-independent model, modeled without reference to distributed objects and remote accessibility, and a target technology that offers remotely accessible objects. Let's assume for the moment that we want the design to use this remote-access technology throughout, so that every access is remote. (We'll consider the more realistic—and efficient—case that some accesses may need to be local in the next chapter.)

In a traditional, code-based, approach to development, we would modify the platform-independent source model to show access to remote objects. This modified model would then be treated as a *design model*, a new target model that contains both the application model information and additional information about the implementation. Some code-driven processes might then treat this new model as the sole expression of the system, which risks swamping the application with implementation detail, and also risks inhibiting its retargeting. Other approaches might retain both the application model and the design model, which risks divergence between the two models.

To avoid these problems, a model-driven approach maintains a separate mapping function that transforms the source model into the target model. This avoids swamping the source (application) model with detail, and it also circumvents the problem of model divergence, because the target (implementation) model is generated. Model transformations can be repeated, and the implementation model regenerated, after some iterative change in the source model without the need to make all of the design decisions over again.

In other words, the two main features of model mappings are *construction* and *synchronization*. Mappings are used to construct target models from source models; because models are derived, they are synchronized by definition. In short, mapping functions represent *repeatable design decisions*.

An Informal Example

As an example of design decisions as mapping functions, let's look at the transition between an analysis model and a design model. Assume that the analysis model contains the elements Bank, Customer, Account, and Transfer, as described on page 49.

Now let's transform this model to a design model. One observation we can make immediately is that some information from the application has to outlive the lifetime of the software system, while others do not. Happily, Enterprise Java Beans (EJBs) provide two forms of beans that correspond to these two needs. An **entity bean** is a remotely accessible object that can live for the lifetime of the software system and whose state is stored in and loaded from an underlying database. A **stateful session bean** is a remotely accessible object that lives for the life of a client session.

The result appears on page 50. This looks fine, doesn't it? But what were the rules and patterns by which we arrived at these decisions for transforming the original analysis model into this model?

Analysis Model Information

- A *Bank*:
  - knows its *Customers* and its *Accounts*
  - can establish and abolish relationships with *Customers*
- A *Customer*
  - knows his or her name
  - can open *Accounts*
  - can close an *Account* he or she owns
  - knows the *Accounts* he or she owns
  - can command the *Transfer* of an amount of money from an *Account* he or she owns to another *Account*
- An *Account*
  - knows its account number
  - knows its balance
  - knows the *Customer* who owns it
  - can withdraw an amount of money from its balance
  - can deposit an amount of money to its balance
- A *Transfer*
  - knows the amount of money to transfer
  - knows its source and target *Accounts*
  - executes by withdrawing the specified amount of money from its source *Account* and depositing it to its target *Account*

With regard to the lifetime of the *Bank* and its *Customers*, *Accounts*, and *Transfers* in the scope of the modeled area of discourse, the analysis model states the following:

- A *Bank* exists for the lifetime of the software system.
- A *Customer* exists from the moment the customer has entered into a relationship with the bank until the moment the *Customer* has closed all of his or her *Accounts* and has quit the relationship with the bank.
- An *Account* exists from the moment it has been opened until the moment it has been closed.
- A *Transfer* exists from the moment it has been commanded by a *Customer* until the moment it has been executed.

Design Model Information

- A *Bank*:
  - is an entity bean with persistent attributes pointing to its *Customers* and *Accounts*
  - has operations for establishing and abolishing relationships with *Customers*
- A *Customer*:
  - is an entity bean with persistent attributes holding his or her name and pointing to his or her *Accounts*
  - has operations for opening and closing *Accounts* and for commanding *Transfers*
- An *Account*:
  - is an entity bean with persistent attributes holding its account number and balance and pointing to its *Customer*
  - has operations for withdrawing and depositing amounts of money
- A *Transfer*:
  - is a stateful session bean with transient attributes holding the amount of money and pointing to the source and target *Accounts*
  - has an operation for executing the transfer

First, we visited the elements of the analysis model one by one and examined their properties. Then, we looked for properties that are expressible in EJB, by digging into our EJB treasure chest and looking for design notions that would best reflect the input model's properties, and then constraining the reasonable choices for dependent model elements once we mapped a model element.

The specific rules we came up with include the following:

- A class whose instances need to persist over the lifetime of the software system shall be represented as an entity bean.
- A class whose instances need to persist for some indeterminate time — shorter than the lifetime of the system but longer than any particular execution of system functions — shall also be represented as an entity bean.
- A class whose instances exist only for a relatively brief period of time, and that carry information relating to entity beans, shall be represented as a stateful session bean.

- Every entity bean and stateful session bean shall have attributes that reflect necessary information about associations in the analysis model.

These rules make up a mapping function, and the particular mapping of the banking system's analysis model is an application of this function. Contrast this with a code-driven development process, where the mapping rules are implicit and lost once executed. As a consequence, they can't be repeated on the same model, nor can they be applied on a model that requires a similar design.

Mapping Functions

A **mapping function** is a collection of rules or algorithms that defines how a particular mapping works. A **mapping** is the application or execution of a mapping function in order to transform one model to another.

Mapping functions are defined against metamodels, but they operate on models. One of the rules stated above was, "Turn every class with at least one persistent attribute into an entity bean." That statement relies not on the specifics of a model, but on related types of model elements, where a *type* denotes a group of model elements with common properties—which is exactly what the metamodel does for us. This explains why we felt compelled to discuss it in the previous chapter. (That, and we really get into this "meta" stuff.) So, the very existence of source and target metamodels is a prerequisite for specifying a mapping function.

A mapping function is not specific to a single model; rather, it applies to all models that conform to the same metamodel, which makes the mapping function reusable.

Mapping functions can be arbitrarily complex. For example, one would treat all elements of an analysis model that call for lifetimes longer than a single execution of the system as belonging to some type associated with "persistence." Going forward, each of these elements would be involved in one or more mapping rules that defines how persistence is going to be realized in a concrete way.

Query, Views, and Transformations (QVT)

To deliver the two main features of model mappings, construction and synchronization, mappings must be executed automatically. This also shortens turnaround times, scales up to large models, and helps avoid manual work, which results in fewer errors and therefore improves overall quality.

Obviously, the rules that define a mapping have to be provided in a machine-readable manner to make them executable. This requires a formalism in which the rules can be expressed; the models must be formalized too, so that they can be consumed and produced by a machine.

Recognition of these facts has led to QVT, for *Query, Views, and Transformations*. There may be several types of QVT when all is said and done, depending on usage. For this reason, we lay out here several approaches to the problem.

The rules or algorithms that constitute a mapping function have to be specified with some formality in order to be subject to automatic execution with correct and reproducible results. Many formalisms are appropriate for this task. The most important approaches are imperative, archetype-based, and declarative.

Specifying a mapping function *imperatively* means implementing all rules and algorithms in a procedural programming language that defines how to query data in one metamodel, transform it, and then write it out. While this is a familiar approach—we're talking an ordinary, boring programming language here—the mapping isn't reversible, so one can't construct the source model from the target. While that may not appear important at first, non-reversible mappings make it more difficult to reverse-engineer models, which can make understanding the target model difficult.

An *archetype-based*[1] approach defines a mapping function as a set of templates that mix code or rules into the text to be generated. This can be implemented as a data access language that selects the appropriate elements from the source metamodel, selects which archetype to use for what source model elements, and then selects how to transform this information into something else that one can then insert into the target model.

---

1. We chose "archetype" so as to distinguish between this concept and C++ templates, which is a related but slightly different concept.

The archetype-based approach is particularly well-suited for generating text from metamodels. The sequential and visible nature of a character stream highlights the importance of order, location, and formatting issues, which are nicely addressed by text-based archetypes.

A *declarative* approach to mapping specifies the algorithms as rules that specify what is to be produced, not how it's done. This approach lends itself much better to automated reversibility of the rules than the imperative approach or the archetype-based approach, though that doesn't guarantee reversibility—the modelers still have to do some work.

Looking ahead, we can envision a *model-driven* approach to specifying a mapping function. The relationship of this approach to any of the approaches we've discussed to this point would basically be the same as the relationship between MDA-driven software development and handcrafting code. After all, surely all of the same reasons for modeling apply to mapping functions as for any other model we build.

Models make it possible to provide formal and rigorous definitions of parts or all of the mapping function, which could then be "filled out" using any one of the approaches outlined above. We view the model-driven approach to specifying mapping functions as the most general, into which the other approaches could be embedded. They could also hide the gory details of the metamodels at each end of the mapping function, as suggested in Weis *et al.* (2003).

Note that a model-driven approach to specifying mapping functions can be recursively applied to itself: One can model the mapping functions that generate mapping functions that eventually produce the system. In other words, this approach can be used to generate generators.

Scenarios for Mappings

Our preceding example mapped an analysis model to a design model, but there are other scenarios for mappings and for mapping functions.

Refining Mappings

We've shown a mapping from an analysis to a design model that changes the level of abstraction at which things are expressed, because the design metamodel has additional language elements. We call such mappings **refining mappings**.

A refining mapping function may create everything needed by the target model, just as a compiler does with C++ or Java programs; in this case, the source model is *complete* in respect to this mapping function. There's no need to examine the target model before executing it or mapping it to the next more detailed model.

There are also scenarios where the mapping function is *incomplete* and it cannot construct everything needed in the target model. This can be overcome in one of two ways: Fill in the blanks in the target model, or associate additional input with the source model in a manner that doesn't pollute it. These techniques may be combined as well. (Chapter 8 discusses how to elaborate models in ways such as these.)

Abstracting Mappings

When we can't see the forest for the trees, it's helpful to abstract stuff away that doesn't add to our understanding of the model or source code. So we can be sure that the abstract view is in synch with the detailed model, we'd like to do it automatically with mappings. Such mappings are called **abstracting mappings**.

Besides providing abstract views on models, abstracting mappings come in handy when moving an existing model to a different platform. An abstracting mapping pulls the contents of the detailed model into a more abstract model whence it can be mapped to other more detailed models for other platforms.

Abstracting and refining mappings are **vertical mappings**, so named because they change the level of abstraction.

Representing Mappings

Sometimes a metamodel is not supported by readily available notations, and sometimes a plethora of metamodels each requires its own notation and tool support. In these cases, we can define a mapping to an existing metamodel for which notations and tool support exist. Such a mapping allows us to create models in one metamodel that stand for models in another metamodel. We call such mappings **representing mappings**.

Representing mappings are most useful when they're reversible. This means that whenever we change the representation, this change is reflected in the represented model, ideally in real time without substantial delay. The reverse is also true: A change in the represented model is reflected in the representation.

An example of a reversible representing mapping is the graphical notation of the UML itself. Any time you change the name label in a class shape of a UML class diagram, a representing mapping running in the background ensures that the name change is reflected in the underlying UML model in the repository. Conversely, if someone changes that class's name using the UML repository's programming interfaces, we'd want this name change to be reflected in all diagrams currently showing this class.

Migrating Mappings

In some cases, porting existing models to other platforms using an abstracting mapping and a refining mapping isn't appropriate because the changes are not substantial. Think, for example, about a migration from one version of a data model to another. Lightweight **migrating mapping** functions can be defined to implement the necessary conversions.

These mappings reformat and regroup existing information to make it amenable to other mappings. Like representing mappings, they don't change the level of abstraction. To contrast these mappings from those that *do* change the level of abstraction, we call them **horizontal mappings**. Other examples of horizontal mappings are optimizations (typically to improve some computational quality like speed, small memory consumption, bandwidth, and so forth) and refactorings (typically to improve some "ility" such as maintainability, readability, and so forth).

Merging Mappings

If a mapping function weaves together aspects of multiple source models to combine them into a single target model, that mapping is called a **merging mapping**. Merging mappings create links between model elements from different models that don't make explicit reference to each other. Figure 5-1 illustrates the concept.

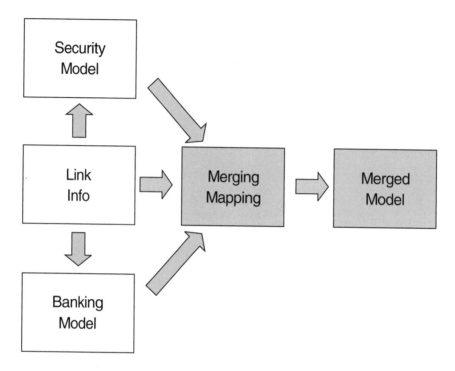

Figure 5-1 Merging mapping

This concept of weaving also appears in the programming language community in *aspect-oriented programming*. Each aspect is a cross-cutting concern, similar to a problem domain, and each aspect is woven together with others by defining a set of merging mappings. We describe how these mappings can be used to weave together Executable UML models in Chapter 9, and we illustrate the mappings in more detail in the next section.

Merging Mappings for Weaving

A function takes one or more input values and produces an output value. For example, the square root function takes a set of real numbers or integers—say, {25, 16, 9}—and generates a different set of real numbers or integers—in this case, {5, 4, 3}. Such a mapping can be stated as a rule (in other words, what we normally think of as a function), or as an enumeration {25:5, 16:4, 9:3}.

This abstruse factoid applies equally to mapping functions. Specification of mapping functions tends to focus on defining rules, but enumerations, while less sexy, are important when a rule can't easily be specified. It may even be the case that it's impossible to specify a rule. Both rules and correlations (enumerations of pairs of elements, one each from the source model and the target model) are both kinds of mapping functions.

For example, assume that a source model for a typical business is to be transformed into a database schema.

- A Customer business entity would correspond with a Customer table that has columns for the Customer's SSN, Name, and Date Of Birth.
- An Address object would correspond with an Address table that has columns for the City, its Postal Code, and the Street.
- An Account business entity would correspond with an Account table that has columns for Account Number and Balance.

To represent the relation between Customers and their Accounts, there would be an additional Account Ownership table, with columns for the SSN of the Customers owning given Accounts and the Account Number of the Accounts owned by some Customers.

The problem is to produce names for the tables and columns in the database. In general, there's no straightforward way of knowing that the Balance column of the Account table corresponds with the Balance attribute of the Account business entity. It might be possible to apply naming heuristics in this example, but that notion will certainly be shredded by real-world database administrators insisting on proven corporate database table-naming schemes. So, we need to correlate the elements in the source model with elements in the target model.

If the database naming convention is to name tables based on the class name and the type of entity (class or relation), then the correlations might look like this:

Source Model Class	Target Model Table
Customer	CustomerTable
Account	AccountTable
AccountOwnership	AccountOwnershipRelation

Similarly, if the convention is to name columns based on a four-character-maximum abbreviation based on the class name, and to limit column names to ten characters in total, then there will be another table that correlates source model attributes to target model columns:

Source Model Attribute	Target Model Column
Customer.Name	Cust_Name
Account.Balance	Acct_Bal
AccountOwnership.SSN	AccOw_SSN

In each table, the left-hand column identifies elements from the source model and the right-hand column captures the corresponding element in the target model.

As usual, the mapping function relies on elements of the metamodel. In the example, then, the mapping function declares a correlation between Attribute on the one hand and Column on the other. The mapping populates this correlation definition with values (Customer.Name, Cust_Name), (Account.Balance, Acct_Bal), and so forth. These correlations define **join points**; see (Mellor and Balcer) for more on this topic. We also provide a more detailed example in Chapter 9.

Using Mappings

We build mapping rules to transform models and to establish links between them. The collection of mapping rules that establishes a mapping between two models constitutes a mapping function. A mapping function is defined against the metamodels of the participating source and target models.

Mapping functions allow us to define and capture design expertise; this is a key contribution of MDA. Mapping functions enable the construction of target models that are necessarily consistent and synchronized with their source models. Because mapping functions are expressed formally, they can be repeated, which allows mapping functions to be used to capture repeatable design decisions.

Mapping rules can't always be applied uniformly. To select which mapping rule to apply in a given situation, model elements can be marked to indicate which rule to apply, a topic we take up in Chapter 6.

Chapter 6

Building Marking Models

In Chapter 5, we observed that mapping functions alone are not always sufficient to transform a source model completely, because we may not be able to select the correct mapping rule based solely on the information contained in the source model and we may need additional inputs to perform the mapping. These additional inputs are provided as **marks**, which are lightweight, nonintrusive extensions to models that capture information required for model transformation without polluting those models.

A **marking model** holds the same relation to marks as metamodels do to models. The marking model defines the names, types, and default values for each mark. Hence, the instances of classes in a marking model are marks; stated in the other direction, marks populate marking models, just as a model populates a metamodel. This chapter discusses what these marks can be, how they are structured, how they connect to model elements, and how they're used by mapping functions.

Why Marks?

Consider the PIM, modeled without reference to distributed objects and remote accessibility, that we introduced in the previous chapter (see An

Informal Example in Chapter 5). A default mapping rule that transforms all object-related source model elements into remotely accessible objects in the target model, just in case there's a need to access them remotely at some time, could yield an implementation that is unacceptably slow. It would instead be more efficient to make some accesses local and others remote.

Of course, there has to be some mechanism that indicates whether to apply the mapping rule that generates a remote access or the mapping rule that generates a local access. The mechanism we use is a mark. Like mapping functions, marks are not part of either the source model or the target model, though they can refer to elements of both models. This separation supports both model portability and longevity.

The separation also provides the ability to evaluate a number of different mapping possibilities without requiring modification of the PIM. This is critical for efficient deployment of enterprise systems, as it allows characteristics like distribution among processors and tasks to be varied while the effects are measured. In embedded systems' design, the same notion of varying characteristics can be applied to associating implementation technology with application models (for example, application elements with a particular task or processor).

An automated mapping could request marking information from the user at mapping time. (One can all too easily imagine an annoying animated paper clip that asks "You seem to be allocating objects. Would you like this access to be remote or local?") However, it's important to store the answer, and thus make it reusable for future applications of the same mapping function to the same source model. This saves the effort of repeatedly and redundantly capturing this additional input (and ridding yourself of that $#@% paper clip again).

Marks can also be derived directly from the source models. For example, we may count how many actions in the Customer class access its Accounts and store that count as a mark. If the count is zero, there's no need to maintain pointers from Customer to Account.

Marks and Marking Models

Several kinds of marks are commonly used; we describe only those associated with model elements of the developer model (at the M1 level; see The Four-

Layer Architecture in Chapter 4) to start with. Based on our example above, each data access operation in the source model would have a mark—we'll call it *AccessorType*—with one of two possible values: **isRemote** and **isLocal**. (We explore how to use the UML's tag definition construct to represent marks in Chapter 7.) As another example, suppose a system will have to handle 100,000 Customers and 500,000 Accounts. This information could be valuable in decisions involving the size of table spaces in a database, and in the generation of optimized data access statements. We can capture this information as a mark *InstanceQuantity* on each class.

Often, a mapping function needs some additional input just because it has to fill a blank in the target model. Imagine, for example, a mapping function that produces a relational database schema from a UML model. Capitulating to the power of today's database administrators, it's a good idea to assume they will tell you the target table and column names, even if there doesn't even seem to be a specific reason for each choice. In this case, the mark is simply used to specify the name of the target table or the column, respectively. The mapping function won't use different rules depending on the mark's value; it simply copies the value to the database schema definition.

We need to define each kind of mark as having a name and a type. In addition, a kind of mark can have a default value.

Consider again the example of producing either remote access or local access from a marked source model. In programmer-esque language:

enum AccessorType [isRemote, isLocal] = isLocal

declares an enumeration named *AccessorType* that can have one of two values, where the default is **isLocal**.

In general, a mark can have any kind of type. For our example of a quantity used to direct table allocation, we could define a mark in the marking model named *InstanceQuantity*, of type Integer, with a default so that the application engineer can choose to enter counts only for those classes with an especially large or small number of instances. We would represent this in our UML model as

InstanceQuantity: Int = 50000;

Similarly, the table name and column name are of type String with no default.

Applying Marks and Marking Models

Mapping functions are the consumers and producers, the sources and the sinks, for marks, but what can a mapping function *do* with all of these marks?

The *AccessorType* mark we described above demonstrates how mapping rules are selected depending on the mark's value. If the value of the mark is **isRemote**, the mapping uses the rules that produce a component enabled for remote access. Otherwise, the rules for local access are used. *Rule selection* is one way in which a mapping function uses marks.

In cases where the mapping function has to fill in a blank in the target model, the mark acts as a *value provider*. As another example, we may decide to postfix certain class names with "_C." This string is a value that would be provided to the mapping function.

Selector marks may also be quantities used to optimize the target implementation. Consider a source model that must be transformed into an implementation that occupies as small an amount of memory as possible. We can save memory if we observe that a particular class has no actions that require references to instances of a related class. For example, if no action ever queries the set of Customers, the Customer class can be marked as *extentLess*, and no container need be generated for instances of that class. By extension, there is no need to generate accessor code.

In some cases, a mark may take on both roles. For example, in an automotive system that assists braking (an ABS), there are only four wheels, there always will be four wheels, and it ain't gonna change. In this case, an efficient implementation may be to construct an array of a fixed size (we're guessing, um, four). Other classes may have different fixed sizes, or may be of variable size on the heap, as usual. In this case, each class will have a mark, *FixedSize*, that, if set to any value other than zero, causes the mapping rule that creates an array to be invoked.

Relating Marks and Model Elements

We've elegantly avoided one critical issue so far: How do we connect the marks to the model elements to which they may pertain?

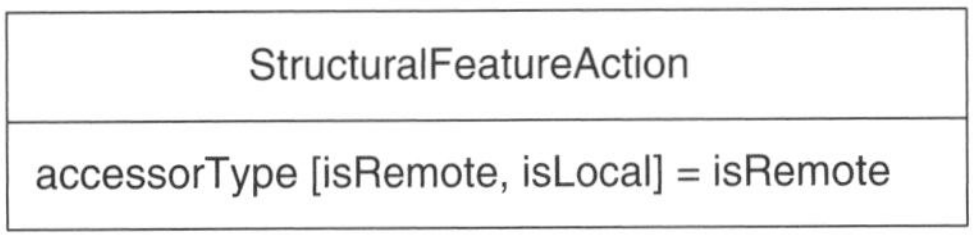

StructuralFeatureAction
accessorType [isRemote, isLocal] = isRemote

Figure 6-1 A very simple marking model

In the remote/local example, the mark only applies to actions that read, write, or clear an attribute. In the UML metamodel, those actions are modeled as a supertype StructuralFeatureAction, and each attribute action can be local or remote. The result is that the mark *AccessorType* is somehow associated with StructuralFeatureAction.

After all this ranting about keeping the marks separate from models, it would be pathological now to pollute the metamodel with marking model concepts. Just as we viewed marks as lightweight, nonintrusive extensions added to the developer model, so too we view the marking model as a plastic sheet laid over the metamodel—specifically, a plastic sheet with an extended attribute of StructuralFeatureAction called *AccessorType*, as shown in Figure 6-1.

This model is intended to convey that the *AccessorType* mark is associated with structural feature (attribute) actions in the source metamodel; each attribute action has a value for the mark. We do not intend to leave the impression that the metamodel should be extended directly. (There *will* be a question about it on the test!) Note that if we were to make the decision between local and remote access for classes as a whole, we would create the mark definition so that it applies to Class model elements instead.

A given model element can have several marks associated with it. For example, consider the transformation of a model into a design expressed in terms of objects that can be stateful or stateless, transient or persistent, local or remotely accessible, identifiable or not. In this case, multiple mapping rules are applicable to each source model element, so there can be marks that enumerate the choices for state, persistence, accessibility, and identity, respectively, to remove this ambiguity. Each of these marks is an extended attribute of the appropriate metamodel class.

The plastic sheet analogy suggests that some marks might be related and could all be placed on the same sheet. For example, a mark *isPersistent* could apply both to classes and attributes, with the implicit rule that any class that has a persistent attribute must also be so marked, so there is a home for the column in the generated table. A single sheet could contain multiple related marks, such as an additional string that describes the target of the persistent data, say **database** or **backup**. Removal of the plastic sheet, then, implies the removal of the entire concept of persistence from the system.

This idea implies that it's useful to consider the reusability of each marking model element: Elements that are likely to be used together by existing and future mapping functions should be grouped together in one marking model. The marks that capture these design decisions can be reused if the source model is transformed into another target model where comparable design decisions would have to be made.

A typical example of the usefulness of marking model grouping is a mapping function that spans multiple platforms. For this example, an ideal marking model partitioning uses two partitions: one for the platform-independent marks and another one for the platform-specific marks. This enables the reuse of the platform-independent marks in the event that the development team chooses another implementation. This also reinforces the idea that portability is an important design criterion when partitioning marking models.

Other Marks

The marks that we've described so far have applied to the elements of a model constructed by the developer, but other kinds of marks exist as well.

For example, we could define a mark "_C" that we postfix to all class names to make it easier to distinguish them from other kinds of elements in the eventual code. This postfix would apply to all classes, not just certain selected classes. As these marks apply to *all* classes that the mapping function transforms, this mark is not linked to any model elements; rather, it is a global configuration mark.

Marks may also apply to instances of classes of the developer models. For example, a telephone system will have some set of classes related to the phones we each use. The instances of those classes need only exist on the switch considered "local" to that phone. Since the instances don't exist explicitly in the developer's model, these instances cannot be marked directly. Instead, they may be described in some manner, using, for example, an area code, or perhaps a separate model will be constructed that provides initialization values for the instances.

Mapping functions can also produce marks for the target model as outputs, which can be useful if the mapping needs to remember how the source and target model elements map to each other. Another useful application of target marks is to allow one mapping to use the output of the other as its input. The target marks of the one are then used as the source marks of the other mapping function. We discuss these chains of mappings in more detail in Chapter 11.

Mark and Marking Model Implementations

There have to be ways for the modeler to assign values to marks. Some implementations provide for graphical drag-and-drop allocation of model elements into folders that correspond with marks; others define an editor for the defined mark sets that can display all marks defined by the model for a selected model element, with pulldown menus for each of the marks. Another option is to define text files, and then use the large set of available editing, scripting, and awk-ing tools.

If the standard specifies a marking model language that can be stored in MOF, then the technology for accessing the marks and their marking models, storing them in a repository, and exchanging them with other tools will be the same as the one used for all other models and metamodels. This will make the sets of marks used by a mapping function just another input model.

The Theory of Marking Models

Today, there's no "theory" of marking models that states exactly what should go into a marking model or how to create one. Indeed, it's not completely cut-and-dried what should be thought of as a mapping, a mark, or a mapping function.

None of this should be a surprise. When we build a program, there are many ways of defining the same behavior, depending on exactly what the developer chooses to parameterize. The same situation obtains here, with the added entertainment that there are several ways to implement marks, marking models, and mapping functions.

As you can see, marks cover a multitude of sins. There is not yet a taxonomy of marks from which we can derive all kinds of marks and know that we are complete. This is as it should be: It's still early in the evolution of MDA. As experience in fully model-driven development grows, the complete range of marks will become clearer, and approaches for when and how to use them (and when and how *not* to use them) will drive us to the next level of understanding and standards. In the meantime, we've described some common or garden varieties.

MDA is utterly relaxed about how marks and marking models will be used, but a good long-term strategy involves making the marks as free of potential implementations as possible. In other words, it's better to describe the instance count for a class, say, than to demand a specific implementation.

Using Marks

We use marks to select mapping rules and to act as inputs to mapping functions. Marks are part of neither source nor target models; they avoid polluting the models so that they can stand alone and be reused in different contexts.

The kinds of marks that can be applied to a model can be captured in a marking model, which defines the salient features of the marks. Sets of marks and their respective marking models go together and may be used to adapt between the respective source and target models.

There are also relationships between marks, such that a mark can be propagated or inherited from one model element to another. Full exploration of techniques that enable effective definition of these relationships awaits the acquisition of further experience.

In Chapter 7, we discuss several approaches to defining languages. These techniques can also be applied to the construction of marking models.

Chapter 7

Building Languages

So far, we've talked about metamodels in a rather abstract manner. It's now time to discuss how metamodels are used to define languages. (This is often done by third parties, so fear not.)

At one level, a metamodel is just a model, so if we wish to define a language, we ought to be able to model it, in UML for example, and away we go. However, the business of writing mapping functions would become impossibly difficult without some commonalities among the various metamodel definitions, so it's helpful to have an agreed-upon subset of the UML; that subset is the MOF.

Building a model for a large language from scratch can be complex and difficult work, and since modeling languages share many common properties, it's unnecessarily expensive. It's sometimes better to subset or extend an existing language. The UML provides another approach to define a language: by extending or subsetting the UML using one or more *profiles*.

A language requires a concrete syntax and tools to manipulate it. In the text-based world, this is easy to do, but in the graphical world, there are fewer tools. By combining the techniques of MOF metamodeling and UML profiles, we show how it is possible (if kludgy) to represent non-UML models using UML.

Whichever approach you use, you're defining a language, so let's start by examining what it is about a language that we need to capture and how we can represent that by a metamodel.

Why Build a Language?

In the normal course of development, you don't always need to build a language explicitly, though you do it implicitly all the time. When you use a subset of the UML for "analysis" and a larger subset for "design," and when you specify what the elements of these subsets actually mean, you have, in fact, defined two new languages, each with a different purpose. It's common to add various adornments to express concepts that don't exist in UML, and to the extent that these things have formal meanings, you have extended the language as well.

In order for the UML to offer support for multiple methodologies, the UML specification says little about how the elements of UML fit together. Consequently, developers or definers of methodologies must determine how to use the various components. You might, for example, decide to use an activity diagram to show how various use cases link together, or build state machine diagrams only for classes and objects. The result of stating such a set of conventions defines one member of the UML "family of languages."

There are two major reasons to *define* a language within the UML family (as opposed to simply using one without saying what it is). The first is communication among team members. For example, some folks on the team might think that persistence is of huge importance to a banking application ("Account balances aren't transient!"), while others might argue that persistence is a design issue. There needs to be agreement on whether to include persistence in a certain model, and on many other issues like it. Similarly, if you decide to add a tag named {persistent} (as opposed to {persistence} or {database} or whatever) within implementation models, you have implied a meaning for that term.

All of these decisions could be enforced by a Notation Police, but this approach is notoriously acrimonious and ineffective. It's better to define the rules in a more formal way, which brings us to our second major reason for defining a UML language: communication with machines. Defining languages formally allows for transformations between models expressed in those languages.

Who Defines a Language?

Anyone can define a language, but for the purposes of discussion, we can divide them into five groups:

- Standards bodies
- Tool vendors
- Methodology definers
- MDA architects
- Developers

Standards bodies, such as the OMG, define languages so that their other standards can have increased usage. An example is the UML profile for CORBA, which describes how to use a subsetted and extended UML that can be transformed into CORBA implementations. (In addition to common platforms such as CORBA, domain-specific task forces also meet within the context of standards bodies to establish a common vocabulary or a common language.) When there's a standard language, users don't need to work this out for themselves each time, and tool vendors can build tools that implement the mappings. The presence of a defined language creates a market, which in turn encourages vendors to build tools, which brings in more users, which increases the size of the market. The result is a virtuous circle that makes the standard that started it all the more useful.

Tool vendors also define languages for much the same reasons. In this case, the existence of a language legitimizes the tooling and brings in customers. Vendors may also need to define a language to exploit certain features of some infrastructure for a customer (for example, if a customer is using a nonstandard object request broker [ORB], or to make use of certain features of the toolset).

Methodology definers define languages because they just can't help themselves. Executable UML, for example, defines a tractable subset of UML, which then becomes the basis for defining a process for effectively building models that developers can apply. Again, the existence of a standard language increases the "reach" of the methodology, which in turn encourages the support of tool vendors—another virtuous circle.

MDA architects who introduce a framework or who want the developers to target a certain proprietary component architecture also often need to invent a language. While not being "standard," such a language helps the developers create the particular system more efficiently. By linking the language to more abstract and standardized languages using mapping functions, the resulting specifications benefit from the general MDA advantages such as portability, which is valuable if you move away from the proprietary frameworks or architectures in the future.

When there's no readily available language, developers may choose to build one. This should be a rare occurrence, because language definition is a time-consuming and abstract task. For a developer defining a language, this means that the effort must pay off and not just be an intellectual exercise. And yes, overall savings can be achieved by the hacking folks coming up with a language and corresponding mapping functions.

The definition of the language does not need to be made explicit, though there are obvious advantages to so doing. Standards bodies have to make the language definition explicit because that is their product, which then raises a question: What's in a language?

What's In a Language?

The structure of a language is different from its concrete syntax. We could, for example, represent classes with clouds or boxes, and states with elongated rectangles or ovals, and it makes no difference to the underlying meaning. Unfortunately, it's difficult to talk about classes and states without a notation, and once a notation becomes established, it's easy to confuse the notation with what it represents. When we talk about building modeling languages, we talk about the "definition of the language," which is expressed as a meta-model.

But what is that "definition of the language?" In OMG-speak, it is the **abstract syntax**, a phrase that captures the idea of the structure of the language, separated from its concrete notational symbols. The UML metamodel doesn't refer to the shapes used to represent the model elements in diagrams, and UML models can even be represented textually, using the Human Usable Textual Notation (HUTN 2002). The metamodel captures only the abstract syntax of a language, but *not* its representation (in other words, its concrete syntaxes).

Which is all rather peculiar, since the graphical notation of the UML is the feature that many people think *is* the UML. This is what comes from confusing the medium with the message.

Building a Language Using MOF

As we wrote in Chapter 4, the M3 level at which MOF resides is a model of the simplest set of concepts required to capture models and metamodels, which means that MOF is *the* surefire way to define metamodels. So long as you only use the set of constructs defined by the MOF—which, while simple, are certainly powerful enough to capture the static structure of a model—you can define the abstract syntax of any modeling language.

If you're familiar with the UML, you're already familiar with the most important concepts of the MOF. Indeed, the UML core is a superset of the MOF metamodel in MOF 2.0 and UML 2.0.

MOF offers five important concepts that you can use to define a language:

- Types (classes, primitive types, and enumerations)
- Generalization
- Attributes
- Associations
- Operations

Figure 7-1 shows the fragment of the UML metamodel that defines a class Comment. This class allows us to create those little sticky notes that we can attach to model elements. As such, Figure 7-1 is a UML model (of the UML).

Figure 7-1 is also a MOF model because it uses only the limited constructs we listed above that are allowed in MOF. Moreover, because the MOF has no concrete syntax, we have expressed the model using UML notation, though we could have chosen any notation at all.

By design, the UML metamodel is expressed entirely using the MOF subset, so any example model fragment would have qualified as a MOF model.

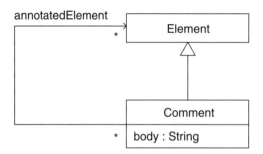

Figure 7-1 Excerpt of UML metamodel in MOF

However, if you were to build a model in UML using, say, an association class, that model would be UML only, and you would have to transform it into the simpler constructs of the MOF for it also to be a MOF model. The association class could be re-expressed as an ordinary class with two separate associations to the primary classes, and this would then conform.

Given the UML as a concrete syntax for MOF, building a MOF model is really "just" building a UML model with a more restricted abstract syntax. Now all you have to worry about is figuring out what the appropriate conceptual entities in your language need to be.

Of course, it's also possible to reuse the whole UML metamodel or parts thereof to derive your own variant. If you're happy with most parts of the UML, but you've always been missing this one concept that you wished the UML designers had thought of, you can create a copy of the UML model and modify it. Although you're diverting from the UML standard, you are reusing a proven modeling language, which is more effective than designing your own language from scratch.

Building a Language Using Profiles

Natural language is extensible; in other words, new notions can be introduced on top of the syntax and vocabulary established so far without the need to learn a new language. Modeling languages also support extensions to their vocabulary so that modelers can express domain-specific notions, rather than be restricted by the more basic and abstract vocabulary of the UML.

On the other hand, other modelers find the vast number of concepts offered by the UML to be over the top, so they'd like to be able to confine the use of the UML to ensure that only concepts required in their environment are used.

You can extend or confine the UML—whichever you need—by creating a UML **profile**, which is a mechanism for adapting an existing metamodel with constructs that are specific to a particular domain, platform, or methodology. Starting with UML 2.0, profiles are now part of UML models, as opposed to being external metadata as they were in UML 1.x.

A profile is constructed using any combination of the two mechanisms described in the following subsections.

Stereotypes

A **stereotype** extends the basic vocabulary of the UML. Stereotypes can be attached to a model element to signify that the element is in some way different from others. For example, we've described some elements of the Bank model as *persistent*, but this fact is not inherent in the bank (try using the word next time you talk to a teller!), nor is it a part of the UML. By assigning a stereotype «persistent» to a model element of, say, type Class, you state that the class is not just a simple class but a persistent one.

Defining a stereotype is similar to creating a subclass of an existing UML type. Figure 7-2 shows an example where the stereotype *persistent* is defined to be applicable to model elements of type Class. The «stereotype» on *persistent* indicates the definition of a stereotype that extends (as shown by the arrow) the metaclass Class—that is, the class Class in the UML metamodel.

With this definition in place, the stereotype «persistent» can only be assigned to model elements of class Class or any of its specializations. If instead you wished to create a stereotype that applies to interfaces as well as classes, you would extend the base class of both Class and Interface, which is Classifier.

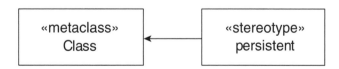

Figure 7-2 Stereotype *persistent* applied to elements of type *Class*

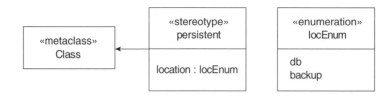

Figure 7-3 Defining an attribute for a stereotype

The definition of a stereotype may include attributes that act as tags.[1] For example, we may decide to store some persistent data in a database and other persistent data in a backup file somewhere. To do this, we can add an attribute to the «persistent» stereotype, say, *location*, which is an enumeration comprising two literals, **db** and **backup**, as shown in Figure 7-3.

Applying a stereotype creates an instance of that stereotype and links it to the given model element. The stereotype's attributes and associations can then be manipulated just like those of a regular class. The top of Figure 7-4 shows how the UML graphical notation displays the attributes of a stereotype. The bottom of the figure shows the same information as an object diagram of the corresponding UML model elements.

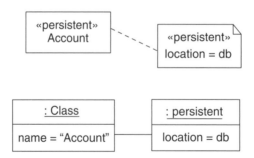

Figure 7-4 Showing values of stereotypes and corresponding instance (object) specifications

---

1. In former times (UML 1.4), stereotypes used to allow for *tagged values*. With UML 2.0, the tagged value is gone. Long live the tagged value! In modern days, stereotypes can define anything a class can define, including attributes and associations. The UML still allows us to refer to the attributes of a stereotype as *tag definitions*, and the values that they assume once the stereotype is applied to a model element as *tagged values*, just for old times' sake.

Constraints

The UML specification defines the abstract syntax of the set of diagrams that comprise it, but as we mentioned before, it doesn't state exactly how these diagrams fit together nor how to fit them together to form a consistent whole. This problem worsens once you've added your own stereotype definitions. The UML allows a language designer to specify formally which elements to make available, though, and how those elements fit together. The mechanism for this is the text-based Object Constraint Language (OCL). (See the sidebar Object Constraint Language (OCL).)

Executable UML, for example, is a subset of UML that uses a simple version of the state machine diagram in which no hierarchical states are allowed. This rule can be stated using OCL by saying that the size of *allInstances( )* of the metaclass Superstate is zero, which neatly makes it "illegal" ever to use a hierarchical state machine. (The function *allInstances( )* is an OCL-supplied function that refers to all of the existing run-time instances of a class.) This is an example of a **well-formedness rule**, which is a rule that specifies a condition that a model must satisfy in order to be "well-formed."

We can also use OCL to define how model elements fit together. In Executable UML, for example, a state machine diagram illustrates the behavior of objects of a class and nothing else. A constraint would assert that the names of the state machine diagrams match only those of classes; in other words, the state machine diagram for "Dog" is legal only if there exists a class named "Dog." (In fact, the rules are a bit more complicated than that, but we'll start with this.)

A state machine diagram can also describe the behavior of the set of objects of a class. (And then there are generalization hierarchies and subtype migration, but you get the idea.) These informal rules can be expressed formally in OCL as well-formedness rules, with the result being a set of constraints over a model.

Constraints also come in handy when you've defined several stereotypes that are related to each other in some way. Say, for example, you've defined one stereotype called «Session», applicable to classes, and another one called «Entity» that's applicable only to those classes that are not stereotyped «Entity». If not otherwise constrained, the UML specification would allow you to assign both stereotypes to a single class at the same time.

Object Constraint Language (OCL)

The **OCL** is a formal language that modelers can use to express conditions that must hold true for the system being modeled. The OCL plays a very important role in the detailed specifications of many elements of the UML.

The OCL is a pure expression language: When an OCL expression is evaluated, it returns a pure value that doesn't cause any side effects.

The concept of well-formedness rules is an application of the OCL. Three OCL constructs address well-formedness rules directly:

- A **precondition** is a condition that must hold true at the moment that execution of a particular operation is about to begin.

- An **invariant** is a condition that must hold true for all instances of a particular model element (such as all objects that belong to a given class).

- A **postcondition** is a condition that must hold true at the moment that execution of an operation has just ended.

OCL expressions generally appear on UML diagrams within notes or the definitions of classes.

There are several good reasons to use the OCL in MDA-related models:

- Constraints are unambiguous, and squeezing out ambiguity is always a good technique for improving the understandability of a model and the ability of team members to communicate about that model.

- Constraints add precision to models.

- Constraints add information about model elements and the relationships among them; this information serves as an excellent form of documentation for the system being modeled.

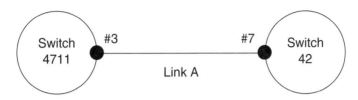

Figure 7-5 A graphical representation of a network

Therefore, you should add an OCL constraint that allows, at most, one of these two stereotypes to be applied to a single class at any time.

The combination of the UML metamodel, a set of stereotypes you define, and a set of constraints over instances in that metamodel—those instances that capture a developer's model—defines a language in the UML language family, the language you wish to use for whatever nefarious purpose you have in mind.

Building Graphical Notations

Imagine you want to be able to draw the model depicted in Figure 7-5. The diagram shows two switches connected with a link; the link is attached to a port on each switch, where the port has a number. We can capture the conceptual entities in this model by constructing the metamodel shown in Figure 7-6.

Defining the metamodel is one thing; having a concrete syntax and notation to use in creating, editing, and maintaining the corresponding models is another. Stated another way, how can we create and edit diagrams like Figure 7-4 and create instances of the classes in the metamodel of Figure 7-6? "Meta-case" tools are one way of creating custom graphical notations for any kind of meta-model, but even they have to connect properly to the important MDA standards to be generally useful.

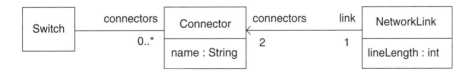

Figure 7-6 Metamodel for network

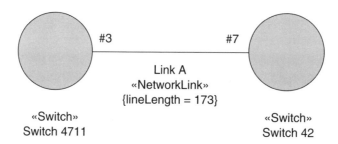

Figure 7-7 UML rendition of metamodel for network

As it happens, we can draw a UML diagram that looks almost like Figure 7-5 using the existing graphical notation for UML. Figure 7-7 shows the resulting UML model. It uses the UML notation for an interface (called "lollipop" notation) with stereotype «Switch» to represent the switches, the graphical notation for an association to represent the link, and association ends to represent the connectors.

Figure 7-8 shows the mappings we have used between the networking metamodel shown in Figure 7-6 and the UML rendition of Figure 7-5 shown in Figure 7-7. This sort of mapping to UML using stereotypes and tagged values can be applied to any metamodel defined in MOF. The general pattern is to find similar structures in UML, use stereotypes to avoid ambiguities, and, if nothing else helps, map the associations in your metamodel to UML dependencies and map attributes in your metamodel to attributes of stereotypes.

The same technique can be used to represent marks and marking models in UML. Typically, a set of mark definitions is mapped to a stereotype that defines an attribute for each mark definition in the set. The attribute's type and default value are set according to the mark definition. The stereotype is defined to apply to the types of model elements to which the set of mark definitions applies.

To ensure that the marks are available on all corresponding model elements, the stereotype can be made mandatory by adding a tag {required}, as shown in Figure 7-9. The resulting mapping is a representing mapping, as discussed in Chapter 5, which acts as an adapter between your metamodel defined in MOF and the UML metamodel.

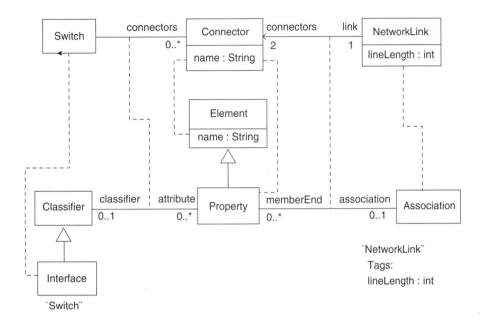

Figure 7-8 Mapping between network and UML metamodels

For the example, a mapping function can rely on MOF and its definitions for how the model can be accessed. It will hold a model element of type Switch and ask it for its connectors, simply by calling *getConnectors()* on that model element. The profile implementation will handle the navigation of the under-lying UML model. (The function *getConnectors()* would be a user-defined function that retrieves all instances of the Connector class associated with the given instance of Switch.)

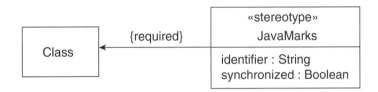

Figure 7-9 Marking stereotype as mandatory

With this tool of UML profiles in hand, we're all set to metamodel away. As the profile implementation provides us with the true view of our concepts, we don't have to hassle with the details of how we represent the model in UML, which could change if the UML version changes. The mapping functions that are based on the underlying metamodel won't be affected by this.

This powerful way of combining MOF metamodels and UML profiles should be used if the metamodel uses substantially different concepts from those offered by the UML. Otherwise, mapping functions would have to concern themselves with stereotypes and tagged values instead of the concepts of the real metamodel. This would make the process of specifying a mapping function tedious and error-prone. Moreover, it would make the mapping function specific to the profile.

Note that this approach of bending a UML tool to build a graphical notation is something of a kludge. New meta-case tools are already starting to appear that provide domain-specific notation, though as we noted earlier, these tools will have more reach if they connect to the MDA tool chain.

Using Languages That You've Built

We build (or use preexisting) languages for the same reasons we build metamodels: to declare the elements of a modeling language so we can build mappings between them. However, construction of a metamodel is only one way to build a language.

The genius of the UML is that it is ecumenical: It allows anyone to use it in any way he or she chooses. A user of the UML has the ability, via the profile mechanism, to add features so that additional meanings can be adduced. Alternatively, you may build a MOF metamodel, either from scratch or by importing the UML metamodel and making incremental variations from that.

A language needs a concrete syntax. One approach is to bend the UML to your will by constructing mappings between the abstract syntax of a UML concrete representation and the metamodel of your language. An alternative is to construct a domain-specific language that meets your specific needs.

Sometimes a language is incomplete, or it requires addition of elements at a different level of abstraction from the rest of the model. In this case, we may elaborate the generated model. We take up this topic in Chapter 8.

Chapter 8

Elaborating Models

MDA allows you to model your problem domain to such a degree that the resulting model is executable without further elaboration. This is usually accomplished through action languages, where such a model can be translated into code with complete control of the generated output. In this scenario, we simply apply the mapping functions and generate the system, rather as we do today with code that we compile. Modelers use mapping functions to (re)create all of the target models from these primordial inputs, and additional inputs for the mapping functions may then appear only in the form of marks.

However, it's not always possible to produce complete models, or the models may not meet all of the nonfunctional requirements of a software development process, such as a cultural need to see a "design" model. More commonly, there can be an impedance mismatch between the source modeling language and the target model that would cause a source model to have to contain elements at radically different levels of abstraction. We may find also that it's not appropriate to put everything in a single model and map it to the target in one step. Consequently, MDA provides for the capability of *elaborating models*.

Model elaboration is the idea that a target model can be modified after it has been generated. Generally, this means adding code to the model, but it can also mean editing or refactoring the generated model in any manner you select. This possibility of target model elaboration is an advantage of the MDA framework because it allows developers to ease into model-driven development, rather than take a step function from a code-driven process to a model-driven development one.

Why Elaborate Models?

There are many scenarios in which we might choose to elaborate a model. The most conspicuous is filling in the implementation of a method generated from an incomplete model. All that can be generated for a method whose semantics aren't captured by the source model is a plain return statement or a "not implemented" exception. Patently, this has to be "elaborated" via the addition of some sensible code.

As another example, when we generate a user interface (UI) from the structure of a model, the generated UI may have to be elaborated to improve layout or improve the UI elements to be used (for example, radio buttons as opposed to a drop-down box), or to address fields that aren't required in a given context. In this case, the source modeling language doesn't explicitly expose all of the artifacts required on the ultimate target, so the target needs to be elaborated.

Next, imagine a business model captured in a modeling language using work-flows, resources, business rules, synchronization points, and the like. Let's assume that we want to map this to a model that addresses implementation components, inheritance, attributes and operations, storage formats, transactions, and so forth. There are several aspects for which the mapping function can only guess default settings, and some of these settings may not even be filled in automatically from what's in the business model. Again, elaboration of the target model is required. This can mean the addition of technical detail required for the implementation of the business model and changing settings wrongly proposed by the mapping function. As in the UI example above, the business modeling language wouldn't have allowed us to provide this kind of specification; moreover, the business model is not the right place to talk about technical implementation detail.

Manual model elaboration, though generally required in practice, represents a break from the "pure" approach of linking models through the application of mapping functions. Though this human intervention is an integral part of MDA, you should use it carefully in order to get the best out of your MDA process.

Here are a few guidelines for deciding whether or not to elaborate:

- Don't elaborate a model if you don't have to; otherwise, developers will have to understand all of the metamodels and mapping functions involved.
- Strive for intuitive and accessible ways of providing specification knowledge.
- Localize elaborations; avoid redundancy in elaborating locations.
- Don't expose intermediate models that don't need elaboration.

Observing these criteria means that model elements are added only at the appropriate level of abstraction, at the places designed to be elaborated.

In addition to the possibility of elaborating a model, we may also wish to expose a model so it can be examined, even if we have no intention of elaborating it. For example, if a model is input to or output from a mapping function that causes a significant change in the level of abstraction, being able to view the mapping inputs and outputs can be a tremendous help in understanding what's going on.

Another cultural occasion is the target model as an important artifact at a process or organization boundary. For example, if the software development process calls for a design model before the implementation can start, this target model has to exist as an explicit artifact for delivery.

To avoid unnecessary meddling with generated models, we could create the intermediate models as read-only artifacts, so they can serve as input for the subsequent mappings and be used as documentation.

Managing Manual Changes to Generated Models

When the target model is regenerated, we need to be certain that the model fragments that have been elaborated (in other words, modified purposefully) aren't replaced by regenerated model fragments or portions of models. A simple approach is the concept of *protected areas*. If an area of the source model is protected, the mapping function can simply preserve the manually-entered contents. However, both the source model and the target model can be polluted by protected area boundary tags (though modern editors can hide them). Moreover, it's difficult to build sophisticated merges that do more than preserve entire protected areas, but if the granularity of the protected areas is chosen appropriately, less sophistication is required than you might expect.

Once you've elaborated a target model, there's the issue of how to deal with these manual modifications when the mapping function has to be executed again due to changes in the source model(s). Of course, the desirable outcome is that all manual modifications are "properly" preserved after executing the mapping function again; the trick, of course, is the definition of "properly."

Consider an incomplete mapping function that accepts a UML source model containing classes with operations, attributes, and associations, and produces a class declaration in an object-oriented programming language for each UML class. For each modeled operation, the mapping function creates a method declaration with a signature, but with empty method contents. Let's assume that the mapping expects the developers to fill in the method bodies in the generated source code instead of specifying them in the UML model.

However, what if the modeler changes the method signature in the model between mappings? Does this mean that the same method body should still be used, which risks the production of uncompilable code because the new signature doesn't match the existing manual implementation body? Or what if the modeler deleted an operation from the model and then created it again? In this case, the operation model element would be viewed as a new entity that doesn't match the existing implementation body. And what should we do with the manually-inserted implementation if the modeler decides to remove the operation from the model?

We can express this challenge in terms of finding out what manual changes have actually occurred. We can see that the following are crucial:

- Detecting manual changes in target models
- Preserving/merging manual changes during mapping
- Avoiding the loss of manually-created information

General solutions to this problem are quite sophisticated, but many boil down to finding differences and merging them ("diff-and-merge"). As with any diff-and-merge algorithm, there are cases that are hard or impossible to resolve automatically. These are called **merge conflicts**. In these cases, the modeler has to determine manually which of the changes are to be merged and how this has to be done. Naturally, the modeler's decision should be retained for later use.

Diffing and merging models using text is tractable, but providing the same level of functionality for complex metamodels expressed in MOF, or for graphical models, is still a subject of research, though a great deal can be achieved even today.

Note that diff-and-merge is not the only technique. Manual changes can also be tagged as such during editing, so that model elements have origin tags that point to the corresponding source model element, and so act as traceability links. Manually added elements don't have origin tags; on regeneration, elements with no origin are just left alone.

Yet another approach is to generate the target so that manual code is separate from the generated code (for example, using inheritance or callbacks).

Reversibility of Mappings

Another topic of interest in this context is reverse engineering and bidirectional synchronization of models. Of particular interest is whether it's advisable to allow the modification of models at lower levels of abstraction such that the changes can be merged into models at higher levels of abstraction.

A one-time use of an abstracting mapping can be of tremendous help when you're getting started with MDA and you have a pile of legacy source code. In such a situation, "MDA-enabling" these sources is a practical way to bring them into the fold.

Similarly, a one-time abstracting mapping can be useful when you're moving an existing model to a different platform. An abstracting mapping pulls the contents of the detailed model into a more abstract model whence it can then be mapped to other more detailed models for other platforms. Figure 8-1 illustrates this approach to porting models.

On the other hand, regular and frequent use of abstracting mappings is somewhat more problematic, especially if corresponding refining mappings produce "fan-out" (from single source model elements to more than one target model element). This brings about the situation in which it's unclear what modifications to a single target model element should mean for the source model element.

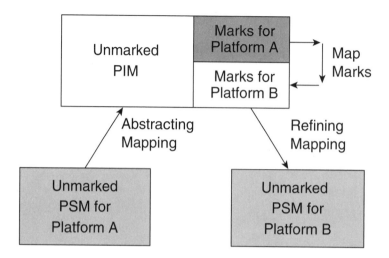

Figure 8-1 Porting models

For example, a model for a multi-tiered application will employ a number of combined mapping functions, one for each tier of the application. Naturally, a change to a source model element will potentially be reflected in each of the tiers (say, presentation, application, and database). To make things more complex, each of these tiers can be divided into a number of layers, such as one for interfaces and another for the classes that implement them.

Now imagine that you change a detail in one artifact and want to apply an abstracting mapping to it.

The trouble is that there are multiple ways to reverse-engineer the type of an attribute—from its member declaration in the implementation class, from the parameter types in getter/setter operations, from entries in deployment descriptors, from column types in database table definitions, from the type of a UI element, and so forth.

In this representative example, mapping functions are *not* reversible without more information. If you require reversible mapping functions, you have to introduce additional rules that account, for example, for the fan-out that occurs during the forward mapping.

Incorporating Legacy Code

In a perfect world, developers and managers alike would realize the benefits of model-driven development and make the switch away from code-driven processes in one graceful step. Magically, legacy code would be transformed into models, and systems' development would proceed apace. Back in the real world, developers—no matter how well-intentioned and eager—cannot immediately acquire model-driven development skills nor the tools to drive the process. And even if those acquisitions were to come to pass, there's still a large legacy of code that cannot be ignored.

Like the primarily graphical models that comprise the UML, code is also a model, in that it's an abstract representation of a subject under study. The issue at hand is to establish how to incorporate this form of model into the architecture of MDA.

There are two main approaches to this issue, though of course there are many approaches in between. One end of the spectrum is to generate code forward to a defined interface; the other is to "harvest" the legacy code and store it in a MOF repository.

When generating code from a model, the generated output is text that can have any desired structure. By marking an operation in a model, the text generated for that operation can conform to the API to some legacy or library code. Essentially, the marks act as a reference to the existing code.

Moreover, should the provided interface prove to be less than attractive, developers can construct wrapper code that presents a more desirable interface, and then generate code to that. This allows the legacy or library code to be manipulated "under the covers" without the need to rethink or repartition the marks on the models.

The other end of the spectrum is to harvest the existing code to create a model and store that as instances in a MOF repository. This brings the legacy code into the MDA fold, where all of the standard techniques can be applied.

Of course, there must still be a mechanism to indicate references to the legacy, and that mechanism, as we described above, is marks.

Using Elaboration

We elaborate models if complete modeling is not possible or if it does not meet all of the nonfunctional requirements of a software development process. In addition, we may elaborate a generated model by reorganizing it.

Protected model areas enable us to regenerate the model at will and so work iteratively. Elaborated models, legacy code, and libraries can be fully integrated into MDA either by generating forward to a (possibly wrapped) API, or by harvesting the existing code and storing it as a MOF metamodel. As always, it's a matter of trade-offs.

Elaboration assumes that the models are incomplete or will require tuning. An alternative approach, which we take up in Chapter 9 and Chapter 10, is to assume that the models are complete.

Chapter 9

Building Executable Models

With the advent of the UML action model, it is now possible to build **executable models**. These models are complete in that they have everything required to produce the desired functionality of a single problem domain. An executable model of a bank, for example, would be able to transfer money from your account to mine (we'll implement the other way later), but it would not have a user interface in a meaningful sense of the word, nor would it have a way of verifying who you are, or even of storing data properly.

Executable models are neither sketches nor blueprints; as their name suggests, models run. This allows us to deliver a running system in small increments in direct communication with customers. In this sense, *executable models act just like code*, though they also provide the ability to interact directly with the customer's subject matter, expressed in the customer's language, which is something code doesn't do well.

Executable models for domains are not exactly the same as code (though they *are* something like aspect-oriented code) because they need to be woven together with other models to produce a system. These other models would include, of course, a meaningful user interface, a way of verifying who you are, and a way to store data properly. However, as each model is complete in itself, once the weaving is done, the system is complete.

Why Executable Models?

Java, Smalltalk, and C++ are at a higher level of abstraction than assembler, but they still call for consideration of a number of concepts of no interest to a customer. In conversing with customers, it's preferable to use a highly abstract modeling language that focuses on a single subject matter—the subject matter of interest to the customer—and yet is specific and concrete enough to be executed. In other words, we need an executable model.

Executable models allow developers to model the underlying semantics of a subject matter without having to worry about, for example, the number of processors, the data-structure organization, or the number of threads. In other words, just as programming languages conferred independence from the *hardware* platform, executable models confer independence from the *software* platform, which makes executable models portable across multiple development environments.

Contrast this with adding code bodies to models. Code bodies are inherently dependent on the structure of the target for which the code is intended. For example, any code written for the target metamodel that assumes remote procedure calls (RPCs) can only be used in an environment that uses RPCs, even if the subject matter captured by the model is banking. The result of this approach is that models are not universal, but instead form silos that mix the modeling language (the metamodel) and the subject matter at hand. This is a form of architectural mismatch (Garlan 1994), which executable models seek to avoid.

Moreover, software platform independence abstracts away glue code required to connect two components implemented using different technologies, such as .NET and J2EE. Executable models therefore enable collaboration between different platforms, as well as projection to arbitrary platforms, which benefits projects supporting multiple iterations, releases, and configurations.

Executable models also provide for early verification. Because the model is executed, it can be shown to be correct (or not) as soon as it's conceived, without waiting for a design or an implementation. We take up this topic in more detail in Chapter 10.

Executable UML

Executable UML (Mellor and Balcer 2002) is a profile of the UML that defines an execution semantics for a carefully selected, streamlined subset of the UML. The subset is computationally complete, so an executable UML model can be directly executed. Modeling rules are enforced not by convention but by execution: Either a model compiles and runs, or it doesn't.

All diagrams (for example, class diagrams, state machine diagrams, and procedure specifications) are projections of an underlying semantic model. UML models that don't support execution, such as use case diagrams, may be used freely to help build the Executable UML models.

The essential components of Executable UML are illustrated in Figure 9-1, which shows a set of classes and objects that use state machines to communicate.

Each state machine has a set of procedures, each of which in turn contains a set of actions. These actions are triggered by the state changes in the state machines that cause synchronization, data access, and functional computations to be executed.

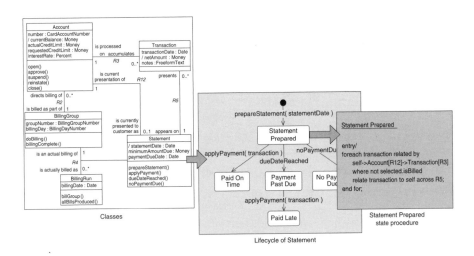

Figure 9-1 Essential elements of Executable UML

A complete set of actions makes UML a computationally complete specification language with a defined abstract syntax for creating objects, sending signals to them, accessing data about instances, and executing general computations. An action language concrete syntax provides the notation for expressing these computations. Because Executable UML is computationally complete, it can be used as a platform-independent language to specify any subject matter in the system.

The difference between an ordinary, boring programming language and a UML action language is analogous to the difference between assembly code and a programming language: They both completely specify the work to be done, but they do so at different levels of language abstraction. Programming languages abstract away details of the *hardware platform* so you can write what needs to be done without having to worry about the number of registers on the target machine, the structure of the stack or how parameters are passed to functions, and so forth. Action languages abstract away details of the *software platform* so you can write what needs to be done without worrying about distribution strategies, list structure, the niceties of remote procedure calls and the like. (See the sidebar Coding Versus Actions.)

As the existence of standards made programs portable across multiple hardware platforms, so too would the existence of an executable UML standard in MDA make models portable across multiple software platforms.

The Execution Model

Figure 9-1 shows the structure of an Executable UML model. However, a language is not meaningful unless there is a well-defined execution semantics. Executable UML has unambiguous rules regarding dynamic behavior—how the language executes at runtime—stated in terms of a set of communicating state machines, which are the only active elements in an Executable UML "program."

Each object and class (potentially) has a state machine that captures, over time, the behavior of that object or class, and associated actions reachable through procedures defined on that object or class. Every state machine is in exactly one state at a time, and all state machines execute concurrently with respect to one another.

Coding Versus Actions

Why use an action language rather than just write code?

The semantics of actions are defined so that data structures can be changed at translation time without affecting the definition of the computation—a critical requirement for translatability (see the next section, Translating Models). Therefore, action models and languages allow you to specify behavior without relying on knowledge of the implementation. For example, a common approach to finding the total amount of the last ten transactions is to loop through the data structure creating a sum as we go. This inextricably links the computation to the data structure, but what if that structure changes? The action semantics casts this example problem instead as two actions: Get the last ten transaction amounts, then sum them. The consequence of this small change in view is that it is possible to change the storage scheme without affecting the algorithm that sums values.

Note that you can use Java or C++ syntax as an action language, so long as it conforms to the underlying action model.

The result is an executable UML model that can be translated to any target.

When a transition fires, a procedure comprising a set of actions is executed. The actions in each procedure execute concurrently unless otherwise constrained by data or control flow; these actions may access data of other objects. It's the proper task of the modeler to specify the correct sequencing and to ensure object data consistency. A state machine synchronizes its behavior with another by sending a signal that's interpreted by the receiver's state machine as an event. On receipt of a signal, a state machine fires a transition and executes a procedure, which is a set of actions that must run to completion before the next event is processed.

State machines communicate only by signals, and signal order is preserved between sender/receiver instance pairs. The rule simply states the desired sequence of activities. When the event causes a transition in the receiver, the procedure in the destination state of the receiver executes *after the action that sent the signal*. This captures desired cause and effect in the system's behavior. It is a wholly separate problem to guarantee that signals do not get out of order, that failed links can be handled, and so forth, just as it's a separate problem to ensure sequential execution of instructions in a parallel machine.

An arbitrary model, therefore, contains the details necessary to support its execution, verification, and validation, independent of implementation. No design details or code need be developed or added for model execution, so formal test cases can be executed against the model to verify that requirements have been properly addressed. This form of verification can be carried out on each executable model, *independent of the other models.*

Them's the rules, but what's really going on is that Executable UML is a concurrent specification language. Rules about synchronization and object data consistency are simply rules for that language, just as in C++ we execute one statement after another and data is accessed one statement at a time. We specify in such a concurrent language so that we may *translate it* onto concurrent, distributed platforms, as well as fully synchronous, single-tasking environments.

Translating Models

Executable UML defines groupings of data and behavior ("classes"), the behavior over time of instances ("state charts"), and precise computational behavior ("actions"). The reason for the quotation marks is that Executable UML does *not* prescribe implementation. Rather, a "class" in Executable UML represents a conceptual grouping of data and behavior that *may* be implemented as a class, or it may be implemented as, say, a C struct and a set of associated functions or as a VHSIC Hardware Description Language (VHDL) entity. (VHSIC stands for Very High Speed Integrated Circuits.) In other words, a "class" doesn't have to be implemented as a class. Consequently, Executable UML is a software-platform-independent language that can be translated into *any* target. For this reason, we also use the word "translatable" as well as "executable."

At system construction time, the conceptual objects are mapped to threads and processors. The generated output must maintain the desired sequencing specified in the application models. Objects may be distributed, sequentialized, even duplicated redundantly or split apart, *so long as the defined behavior is preserved.*

In addition to successive transformation of complete models, models need to be woven together with other models to produce a system. In a banking system, the Bank model could be expressed as an executable model, but it would not solve the bank's problem until it was connected to another complete model of the Security subject matter. When linked together and translated into code, the executable models become a system.

To effect this combination, we can define a mapping function. (This mapping is generally a merging or representing mapping, rather then the refining mappings that transform a model from one form to another. See Scenarios for Mappings in Chapter 5.)

Specifically, we need to establish that one kind of thing in one model corresponds with another kind of thing in another model. For example, the class Customer in the Bank model corresponds with an instance of a Role in the Security model. Another example is that each Account instance in the Bank corresponds with an instance of ProtectedResource in Security. We present the domain-level class diagram for the Security model again for your reference (see Figure 9-2).

Both of these examples are static in that a (static) class in one model becomes an instance in another. (In this sense, the Security model is "meta" to the bank application, even though they both use the same Executable UML profile.)

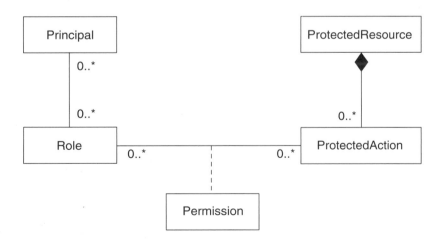

Figure 9-2 Domain-level class diagram for security domain

However, mappings can be between any two kinds of identifiable entity in an Executable UML model. Signals may be mapped to function calls and vice versa; functions can map to changes in attribute values; signals can map to operation calls; actions can map to attributes.

For example, there's a mapping between the Bank and Security models in that a *withdraw* operation must be authorized. Multiple entities may examine a customer's account balance, but only the customer may make a withdrawal. This mapping would require making Account.balance an instance of ProtectedResource and correlating each occurrence of the accessor function that accesses Account.Balance with a ProtectedAction.

As another example, the bank application links to a UI. The user, a teller perhaps, has a screen that allows the customer to make a withdrawal. In the Bank model, this involves the setting of a value for an attribute, Account.Balance. The UI could have been constructed so that a field receives a signal, along with a data value, that causes it to display the value in green if it's positive and red if it's zero or negative. In this example, there's a correlation between an accessor function in the source model and a signal in the target model. Similarly, the detection of a button push in the UI could be modeled in that interface as a function (a signal generator) that maps via a callback function to the reception of a signal in the application. In this case, the correlation is between a signal generator and a signal.

These "further out" examples illustrate the difference between MDA concepts and defining interfaces to components and frameworks via an API. In MDA, the interfaces between models are not defined in concrete; instead, "meta-interfaces" are exported by marking models (the subject of Chapter 6). Because mapping functions act as adapters between models, the fact that the user interface requires a signal to change the value of a field says nothing about the structure of its client.

This sets MDA apart from components and their big brother, frameworks, because the "glue code" we mentioned in Chapter 1 (see Raising the Level of Reuse) is no longer embedded in low-level-of-abstraction-and-hard-to-reuse code.[1] Instead, the rules for mappings are externalized and generalized, which means that they can be applied at will to similar problems.

---

1. MDA is not the first to deploy meta-interfaces. COM, DCOM, OLE, ActiveX, and JavaBeans share some of these properties.

In any case, once these mappings are defined, we're ready to combine all of the models into a single target model from which code can be generated. (These steps can take place simultaneously.) The mechanism responsible is a model compiler, which weaves together the several models according to a single set of architectural rules.

Model Compilers

A **model compiler** takes a set of marked Executable UML models and weaves them together according to a *consistent set of rules*, thus normalizing all of the models to a single common infrastructure. This task involves executing the mapping functions between the various source and target models to produce a single all-encompassing model repository that includes all of the structure, behavior, and logic—everything—in the system.

The final mappings from a model into code can be performed using archetypes, which are especially suited to manipulating text. The archetype-based approach is explained in Query, Views, and Transformations (QVT) in Chapter 5. It remains to be seen whether the adopted QVT standard will be sufficiently general to cover this special case of metamodel-to-text as well as metamodel-to-metamodel. If not, a new MDA standard will have to be proposed.

Whatever the standard proposes, archetype languages must be able to traverse the repository and generate text. The text can be anything at all, including natural language or graphic instructions, but most likely it will be text that can be compiled, such as Java, C++, VHDL, or COBOL.

Marks (see Chapter 6) may be used to provide for point optimization. A mapping function may be defined to provide a different implementation when a particular (marked) region of the model requires it. Moreover, marks can be used to direct the invocation of a mapping function that copies hand-written code, and so incorporate it when required.

A marking model defines a projection on a (source) metamodel. Archetypes and marks that operate on a combination of source models can then be written without any need to determine which archetypes to run, because the projection will have selected the correct model elements. Archetypes can also explicitly refer to the APIs for libraries or legacy code; this provides a way to incorporate these code elements into the overall MDA architecture.

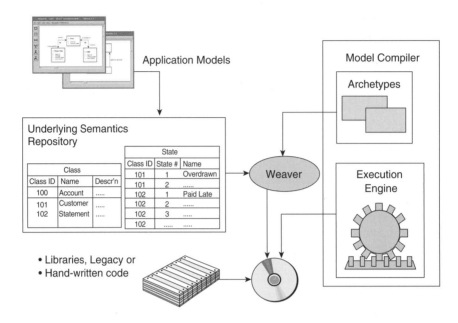

Figure 9-3 Relation between application and model compiler

In addition to mapping all of the source models, the model compiler must also incorporate elements required to execute the models, such as ways to store instances, generate calls and signals across task and processor boundaries, and traverse state machines. These elements, taken together, constitute an Executable UML execution engine targeted to a selected software platform. The execution engine is therefore an implementation of a virtual machine.

The overall scheme (without the additional complexities of marks) is shown in Figure 9-3.

A model compiler imposes a single architectural structure on the system as a whole. Because each executable model is a PIM, and the model compiler compiles the models to make code, you might ask what happened to the PSM. The PSM is there alright—it's the code. Code is a weaving together of the elements of the PIM and of the required platforms, and it executes, too. Using executable models, there's no need to manipulate the PSM or to visualize it as a model. We can go straight to the code, the Mother of All PSMs.

Using Executable UML

We use Executable UML to build a complete model of a single subject matter. Executable UML has a defined semantics for an execution model, which enables the construction of models that can be verified directly in advance of further system design or coding.

Executable UML models are also translatable into multiple software platforms. Archetypes provide for complete flexibility in the structure of the generated code by weaving together execution engine components, legacy code, and application models. Marks, in addition to their normal role of directing the selection of mapping rules, may also be used to incorporate point optimizations and hand-written code. A model compiler targets a specific software platform, optimized to meet the performance properties of the application models.

The direct execution provided by Executable UML enables an agile process, in which a model can be built and executed in cahoots with a customer. We take up this process in Chapter 10.

Chapter 10

Agile MDA

Agile MDA is based on the notion that code and executable models are operationally the same. An executable model, because it is executable, can be constructed, run, tested, and modified in short incremental, iterative cycles. Hence, the principles of the Agile Alliance can be applied equally to models.

Many of the principles of XP and the Agile Alliance involve process and customer relationships and their management, not code. As such, the agile process principles for the construction of code apply just as well for the construction of executable models. For those principles that do specifically mention "code" or "software," an executable model, under this definition, *is* code.

To reach this happy state, models must be complete enough that they can be executed standing alone. Each model in a given set necessarily conforms to the same metamodel, because all models are equal—there are no "analysis" or "design" models. Models are linked together, rather than transformed, and all of them are then mapped to a single combined model that's subsequently translated into code according to a single system architecture.

Why Agile MDA?

To some, the notion of putting "agile" and "modeling" in the same sentence makes no sense. The modelers worry that "agile" is a synonym for "hacker" in its most pejorative sense, while the agilists see lumbering heavyweight processes (and quite possibly lumbering heavyweight methodologists) that deliver the wrong system late at great expense.

The conflict between the modelers and agile programmers is perceived to be fundamental and large, partly because of differing technical focus—"extreme" is an explicit reaction to deliberate processes—and partly because of hype. Yet in reality the gap is quite small. Many of the good ideas of the Agile Alliance and XP (such as Sustainable Development, Estimate to Improve, and, especially, Customer on Site) are equally good in the context of models, and we can simply replace the word "code" with "executable model." Enough, anyway, that one of your authors could become a signatory to the Agile Manifesto in good conscience.

One root cause for this disconnect is the recognition of the *verification gap*. This gap comes about when we write documents that can't execute. Certainly, we can review them and draw conclusions about their correctness, but until we have something that runs, we can't know for a fact that they really do exactly what is needed. Moreover, in the time it takes to deliver a solution, the market and the technology may have moved on, which might make the delivered system, even if it's correct, irrelevant. Worse, some systems are "wicked," in that the existence of a solution changes the (perception of the) problem, which makes the effort to produce a complete and detailed specification document somewhat futile.

Agile methods propose to address these problems by delivering small slices of working code as soon as possible. This working functionality is immediately useful to the customer, and it can be interacted with, which might result in improved understanding of the system that needs to be built. As these delivery cycles can be short (say, a week or two), the systems' development process is able to adapt to changing conditions and deliver just what the customer wants. This eliminates the verification gap.

Because the language of a model is closer to the language of the customer, this enables deeper involvement of customers in reviewing the models. While you can't accomplish much of anything useful by having customers stare at code, you *can* get them to find flaws in your abstractions by explaining to them the models you're using to represent their world.

Agile MDA employs executable models, not code, as the primary artifact. Executable models are more abstract than code, though, which means that these models enhance communications with customers and improve the ability to interact with the customer's domain. Code does that too—that's a primary reason for the focus on it within agile methods—but even high-level languages involve consideration of concepts of little interest to a customer: list structure, distribution strategies, the niceties of remote procedure calls, and the like.

Agile Methods

Agile methods are, in some measure, a reaction to the excesses of deliberate methods that place more emphasis on ceremony (checking those steps off and reviewing those documents) than on the content of software delivery. These methods are called "agile" because "extreme" can be seen as, er, extreme, while "lightweight" is too, well, lightweight. The best known of these methods is XP.[1] Others include Cockburn's Crystal Family, SCRUM, and DSDM.

Some proponents of agile development met in 2001 to form the Agile Alliance.[2] The primary output of this meeting was the Agile Manifesto, which begins, "We are uncovering better ways of developing software by doing it and helping others do it." It then asserts four "value statements" of the form "We value: <left> over <right>." The key point here is not that <right> is bad, but that <left> deserves more emphasis.

Let's look at the four value statements in turn.

Individuals and interactions over processes and tools. Processes and tools are not silver bullets—not even model-driven development and MDA. You can build a system without processes and tools, but you can't build a system without people. And the better the people, the better the result—by far. None of this is to say that process and tools are unimportant; the point is that people and their interactions need to be valued more.

The focus on interactions also emphasizes that using documents, even models, as a one-way interface between people reduces the bandwidth of the communication and increases the likelihood of error.

---

1. See *Extreme Programming Explained* by Kent Beck (2000).
2. For information on the Agile Alliance, see their website, *www.aanpo.org*.

Working software over comprehensive documentation. If you intend to drive to the local hospital, you wouldn't write a document that says exactly how to do it first. Certainly, you need a map that lays out the most effective way to do the task, and you should listen to the radio for up-to-the-minute information on whether a particular route is blocked, but documenting the intended route first is unlikely to stop the bleeding.

Taken literally, preferring working software is unassailable. How could anyone prefer to have a document instead? But there's a subtext here: Is documentation unimportant? Unnecessary? A hindrance? This subtext has led to the deprecation of models and modeling in general, though how one interprets that depends on what one means exactly by a model, a topic we take up in the next section.

Customer collaboration over contract negotiation. We've all heard of projects where the spec has been "frozen," often with unfortunate results. To increase customer involvement, agile processes encourage customer participation even during development.

To eliminate the verification gap and enable immediate delivery of fragments of the system, what we need is a highly abstract modeling language that focuses on a single subject matter—the subject matter of interest to the customer—and yet is specific and concrete enough to be executed. In other words, we need an *executable model*. This executable model abstracts from concrete programming languages, such as Java *et al.*, and in the parlance of MDA, it is platform independent.

Responding to change over following a plan. A plan tells us how to get from where we are to where we're going, but it doesn't tell us if where we're going is the right place to be. If the plan is correct today, it doesn't mean it's going to be right tomorrow. Technology and markets change far too quickly for that. Achieving the plan milestones doesn't necessarily relate to customer success.

This value statement distinguishes *predictive* and *adaptive* approaches. In the construction industry, execution of the plan—the construction phase—takes relatively longer than the planning and design phases. We use the plan to predict when the project will be complete. In software, the design and coding phases take much longer than execution. Even if we define "execution" to be the act of writing code, it is still a small percentage of the total time in the project. Consequently, the plan doesn't predict much of value. Instead, we must recognize that we must adapt as circumstances change.

As usual, this is *not* to denigrate having a plan. Plans for software projects should include *all* phases, not just planning for coding. If interaction with the customer is included during the early phase(s), then the plan should also include time for these interactions. In fact, if you value responding to change, you had better darn well plan for it. The key here is to exploit change to ensure that the product is as close as possible to what the customers need. Reality provides real feedback.

Models, Models, Models

There are at least three meanings of "model," and each one implies diverse usages and connotes different processes.

One meaning for the word "model" is a *sketch*. For example, we might sketch out the shape of a wing on the back of a beer mat, show a few lines indicating air flow, and write an equation or two describing how the two interact. The sketch is not precise or complete, nor is it intended to be. The purpose of the sketch is to try out an idea. The sketch is neither maintained nor delivered. Agile exponents are willing to sketch out classes and use cases (the latter are akin to "user stories") and perhaps even use the UML to do it. There's no fight here: Even the most extreme folk use sketches to outline their ideas for the code.

A second meaning for the word is the model as *blueprint*. A physical model of an airplane in a wind tunnel is one example. More commonly, we think of a blueprint as a document describing properties needed to build the real thing. In other words, the blueprint is the embodiment of a plan for construction.

The connotation of model-as-blueprint causes conflict. The very idea of a "blueprint" evokes images of factories and manufacturing, together with uncreative drones. In an environment that's 80% construction and 20% design, it makes sense to view the blueprint as the plan that is predictive of the construction work to be done. "Heavyweight" processes have encouraged the idea of model as blueprint; the manufacturing analogy is drawn repeatedly in the Software Engineering Institute's Capability Maturity Model (CMM; see *http://www.sei.cmu.edu/cmm/cmm.html*), for example. But we know software is a creative new-economy notion, not at all like old-fashioned manufacturing. To the contrary, software is known for its creative aspects, more like 80% design and 20% construction. In this case, developers need to be adaptive rather than predictive in their relationship to models, which effectively puts the kibosh on the use of models as blueprints.

The third meaning for the word is the model as an *executable*. The model of the airplane can be transformed into the real, physical airplane. When we build an executable UML model, we have described the behavior of our system just as surely as we would have had we written a program in Java. Indeed, when you have a software model that can be compiled and executed within the confines of the functional and nonfunctional requirements, there's no need to distinguish between the model and the "real thing." That's the special property of the software realm.

Consequently, executable models, because they can be automatically translated into code, are as suitable for agile processes as code. Moreover, the degree of abstraction introduced by models is more suitable for what agile processes strive to achieve: bridging the gap between customer and developer, and rapid feedback to verify that the developed system is correct.

Design-Time Interoperability Revisited

Agile MDA expects the construction of various PIMs using the same Executable UML profile throughout (see Chapter 9). The mappings merge models together using the same metamodel because each model conforms to that same profile. This reduces the problem of defining the mapping rules to a simpler and more general problem of defining mappings between model elements in the *meta*model of the Executable UML profile—for example, a state in one domain to an enumerated value of an attribute, or a signal in one domain to a signal in another.

Linking the models together then becomes a matter of indicating which of the elements in each model participate in the mapping. For example, (state) **Overdrawn** in the Bank might match up with (enumerated attribute value) Icon(47).color=**Red** in the UI, while (signal) Button(3) in the UI might match up with (signal) depositMoney to Account 454647 in the Bank domain.

By using a single profile, we avoid silos of transformations that perforce must know something about the structure of each different target metamodel. Any model, then, can be plugged into a design time bus, as suggested by Figure 10-1. This improves design-time interoperability, because all models are equal.

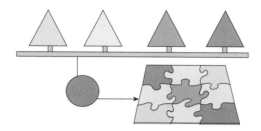

Figure 10-1 A design-time interoperability bus

Except one. The model compiler traverses a single combined repository that contains the merged information from other models, and then executes mapping rules to produce text, the most interesting and useful PSM of them all: code.

Using Agile MDA

We use agile MDA to gain direct feedback from customers about the product under development. We build test cases, write executable models, compile the models using a model compiler, run the test cases, and deliver fragments of the system to the customer incrementally. This is just the same as "We build test cases, write code, compile the code using a language compiler, run the test cases, and deliver fragments of the system to the customer incrementally," except that we've replaced one language (code), with another at a higher level of abstraction: an executable and translatable model.

An executable model, because it *is* executable, can be constructed, run, tested, and modified in short incremental, iterative cycles. Turnaround cycles using models don't have to be longer than coding, because models are transformed automatically into the system. Second, models are not useless or ancillary documents—they *are* the system. As a result of these two, producing executable models doesn't have to be any more heavyweight than writing code, given an adequate MDA infrastructure.

Agile MDA is one possible process for constructing models and linking them together. This leaves open the question of which models to build, which mapping functions are required, and what marking models to apply. Working all that out is the construction and definition of an MDA process, which we take up in the next chapter.

Chapter 11

Building an MDA Process

So far, we have mostly described an MDA process in terms of a single hop from one or more source models to a single target model. Of course, systems these days are often too complex to be transformed in a single hop, and we need to break down the mapping into several hops. The output of each hop, including the target models and the associated marks, can serve as inputs to other mappings. When we link two sets of mappings together, we have a *mapping chain*.

A **mapping chain** comprises a series of what we might think of as stepping stones. Each stone represents a model you've selected; each step from one stone to another represents a mapping function. The path from one side to the other, then, constitutes a particular mapping chain for your project. Deciding where to place the stones, and planning the journey from one side to the other, constitutes a definition for an **MDA process**.

Why Build an MDA Process?

The purpose of defining an MDA process is to determine the domains and bridges, as expressed by models and mapping functions with their associated marks. For each model, we will follow a process that establishes how to go about constructing a good model, reviewing it, testing it, and so forth.

Similarly, the tasks of building mapping functions and marking models have separate processes associated with them. These processes can be determined before or after the overall MDA process is established. The MDA process determines only to *which* models and *which* mapping functions each individual process applies.

Note that careful selection of the models, combined with the splitting apart of complex mapping chains into multiple hops, increases the reusability, portability, and longevity of both models and mapping chains for use in future projects. More immediately, you need a planned process for the project at hand, in which all of the players know which models to build and which can be reused, which mapping functions to build and which can be reused, and how to make use of legacy code.

How to Approach the Problem

Vertical mappings (see Abstracting Mappings in Chapter 5) can be classified in terms of the change in the level of abstraction that they bring about. A **short-hop mapping** doesn't have much effect on the level of abstraction between source model and target model. There's often a fairly clear, nearly one-to-one mapping between elements in the source and target models. For example, a mapping function that turns a class model into a corresponding set of implementation classes, operations to methods, and attributes to members represents a short hop. A **long-hop mapping**, on the other hand, does result in a significant change in abstraction level. An example is a mapping that takes the elements of a model and maps them directly to bits.

There are two ways to approach building an MDA process. One approach is to focus on finding models that exist at a single level of subject-matter abstraction. The other approach is to focus on the length of the mapping chain and find an optimal length for each hop in the chain. Unsurprisingly, you need to use a combination of both approaches.

It's generally the case that long-hop mappings lend themselves to partitioning into a mapping chain comprised of several short-hop mappings. The long-hop example above could be broken down so we map the source model to a specific model that knows about, say, local interfaces and remote interfaces, and then map *that* model to the source code. Not only does the multiple-hop approach simplify the mapping functions; it also exposes the intermediate model so the mapping functions can be reused. The trick is to find good trade-offs among the portability of the models you can create, the traceability and reusability of the mapping functions, and efficient notations for the things you have to specify for the platforms you're targeting.

Charting the MDA Process

Of course, you must identify the models—the stepping stones—comprising your system as part of defining an MDA process. While we can build a model of anything we please, models based on subject-matter boundaries increase the likelihood of reuse of the models.

Some subject matters are easy to find. For example, a user interface is obviously separate from the bank, and it can be modeled as an independent entity. Others are less obvious.

Security, after all, *could* be modeled as a part of the bank application proper. After all, security is a fundamental part of any bank. Indeed, one could make the argument that building the bank-plus-security as a single unit is easier because we can see how security fits in to the bank, and we don't have to mess with mapping functions. On the other hand, a fully developed model of security could be reused for other applications, and the security model could be replaced by a different approach to security. Both models are independent of one another.

Maintaining subject-matter separation makes true model portability possible, though it does require some abstraction work. It is typical, though wrong, to see physical implementation technology built into a model. For example, were we to build an automated teller machine (ATM), it would be a separate subject matter from the task of moving virtual money from one account to another. The right approach is to abstract out a separate problem domain that manages the physical hardware used to control the device, in this case a digital I/O interface that maps directly to events on the application.

The collection of problem domains and mapping functions comprising the system can be depicted by a **domain chart**. Figure 11-1 is a typical domain chart that shows the domains and the bridges between them.

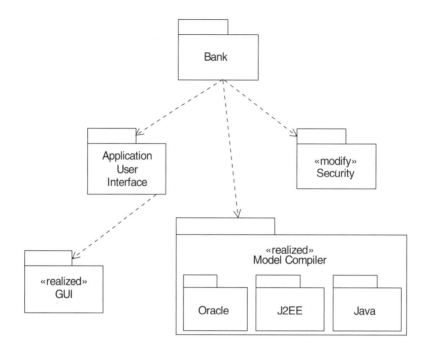

Figure 11-1 Example domain chart

The domain chart provides the foundation for defining the MDA process for your project. (Note that a package that contains all of the packages in the figure via a composition relationship would form a composed realization, which we discussed in Chapter 2 [see Metamodels and Platforms].) The construction and maintenance of this chart provides a framework for continued work on the project, in terms of addressing questions such as, Which models are complete? Which mapping functions? Which metamodels? And which marking models?

Identifying Models

When selecting problem domains from "thin air," it's best to choose domains that separate cross-cutting concerns into separate subject matters, because this will maximize the independence and reusability of each one. Indeed, many of the successful platforms you already have on hand will already be based on subject matter partitioning. It's also the case that these subject matters are typically aligned along the lines of expected changes.

Assuming the preexistence of several models from which to choose, this is primarily a matter of deciding which ones best fit your overall system. Certainly, within your specific vertical market, you're likely to develop a substantial library of platforms that you can reuse repeatedly.

Other platforms that act as services, like Security, may already exist, so perhaps you can immediately reuse them, or you may need to modify them somewhat before they can be harnessed for your application. You may even have to invent them from scratch, though as the MDA market matures, this will become less and less common.

Still other subject matters may exist as code. The domain chart (Figure 11-1) shows these annotated to indicate whether each domain is realized and whether it requires modification.

In addition, editability has to be designed into the model chain explicitly; edited fragments will have to be retained across several regeneration runs of the edited model. Today, there's no MDA standard for the stereotypes we have used here, nor even for the domain chart. Another standardization task!

Identifying the Metamodels and Marking Models

For each problem domain you've identified, you must identify the metamodel that you want to use for modeling. That is, you must identify the modeling language you want to use to capture formalized knowledge models for each of your domains. In the general case, this language can be any profile of any defined language that can be captured in such a way that it can be transformed.

For example, you may choose to formalize knowledge of a bank without thinking about security of certain transactions or remotely accessible objects. In making this choice—a set of assumptions, really—you've defined a modeling language for the construction of the bank. You'll have to make the same decisions for each model you've identified.

Note that each such assumption becomes a requirement on some domain on which you depend. If you "assume away" the problem of security, for example, then something, somehow, has to take on this job.

When you arrange multiple mapping functions into a chain, the source and target metamodels have to match, as do the marking models that each mapping in the chain uses. The mapping chain should be able to operate solely from defined models, mapping chains, and marks supplied by the developer. Mapping functions should produce all marks that the subsequent mappings along the chain require as input. This implies that the marking models match up.

The interfaces exposed by the targeted platforms are those you will implement against. For example, your model should look the same no matter which operating system you intend to use, because you're using a defined API. The mapping functions and associated marking models, then, transform to those APIs.

The Long and the Short of Mapping Chains

Choosing the right combination and granularity of mapping functions is an important and creative process that often involves difficult trade-offs. So, how does one decide? There are multiple factors, but first, let's just deal with the "length" of the link.

Constructing mapping chains from several short-hop mappings can be especially useful if one can combine existing mapping functions into a larger, more powerful mapping function. This is particularly true if reuse of mapping functions generates revenue (either the fiscal kind or the "reputational" kind).

Short-hop mappings can also help in avoiding redundancies that can occur in long-hop mappings. For example, consider a model whose objects communicate without knowledge of distribution. A single long hop would have to build a single mapping function that took a mark indicating whether a given component is local or remote, and then generate the code. Of course, there will be a good deal of commonality between local classes and classes with proxies, yet that commonality is not explicitly exploited. Rather, it's hidden inside the mapping function. We could instead build an explicit intermediate metamodel containing remote and local accesses; build a mapping function that knows about local and remote access; and then build another mapping function that generates the classes.

These metamodels can simplify the individual mapping functions, even to the extent that the effort to implement multiple, simpler mappings becomes less than the effort to implement one long-hop mapping. It's also more likely that a short-hop mapping can be reused in other contexts, whereas a long-hop mapping is specific to its source and target metamodels.

A viable option is to arrange a number of metamodels in an **abstraction hierarchy**, a tree within which the leaves are the metamodels for the target platforms and each of the nodes factors out all commonalities of the metamodels from which they abstract. In this case, each mapping function only has to implement the relatively small steps between metamodels. The mapping functions, and the metamodels on which they depend, are then portable across projects. The domain chart of Figure 11-1 shows an example of an abstraction hierarchy.

The good thing about building up this hierarchy is that once a single reasonable path has been defined for one particular target platform that should be addressed first, one doesn't have to design all of the other metamodels of the tree before anything can get started. If you have a model for some abstract component-based platform that can be realized on top of either J2EE or .NET, say, it's better to take two hops, first from the business model to the component-based model and then on to J2EE source code or a J2EE model. This way, you can start development for J2EE, and simply plug in the .NET model later.

Constraint Propagation and Verification

When one is combining mapping functions by executing them in sequence, the sequence of transformation steps will only succeed if all models produced as outputs by a mapping are well-formed with regard to the associated mapping function. It's desirable to anticipate possible violations up front and to inform the modeler about them. This requires a holistic view of the sequence of mapping functions to be applied, which results in a back-propagation of constraints of mapping functions further down the sequence to verification steps that take place before the mapping sequence is started.

A constraint may take the form of a naming convention or a limitation on the values of a certain element of the target metamodel. Inheritance rules also qualify as constraints; for example, Java allows only single implementation inheritance. Such constraints should be checked as early as possible in the mapping chain, which will in turn enable the modelers to avoid extra effort and errors later in the process of mapping models.

Looking at this another way, this means that constraints in target metamodels should be propagated back up the metamodel chain as far as possible. The issue here is *not* to force the application expert (for instance, a banker) to be aware of implementation technology restrictions; the issue, rather, is to find a place in the process where the restriction can be resolved. Only when it can't be resolved should the expert be aware of the restriction. Ideally, the tools for creating and editing the source models enforce these constraints. If this isn't possible, at least automatic model verification—which the modeler would have to trigger explicitly—should be supported.

A subtler form of constraint comes about when assumptions are not met by a dependent domain. For example, if the Bank assumes the existence of a Security domain that protects specific operations, but the developers of the Bank model only provide for identity verification, then there is missing functionality in the system.

Using an MDA Process

We build an MDA process so that we know what models to build, which mapping functions are required, and what marking models to apply. This MDA process for your project is a living entity; as your understanding of the system grows, the choice of models and links between them may change and grow. It provides a framework for the work that needs to be done, and it can be used to capture revised understanding and act as overall top-down plan for the project. You have to have a plan so you can change it.

Chapter 12 takes up the topic of using the MDA process you have built.

Chapter 12

Executing an MDA Process

This chapter describes a model-driven development process in terms of the key activities and their interdependencies. We begin by describing the main activities for a simplified system in which there is a single application source model and a single target implementation model, both of which apply to a single platform. We then expand the discussion to cover the issues involved in iterating a specific process in the presence of multiple platforms.

Broadly speaking, we developers carry out two main activities. First, we formalize knowledge of a subject matter, and then we render that knowledge as an implementation. In MDA, one carries out this activity by building a model of a platform in a modeling language that can be transformed into others. The second activity is to map that formalized knowledge onto a target platform to create a system.

System development should, of course, take place in an iterative, incremental fashion. Thus, there will be repetition of these two basic activities on succeeding increments of the system, and sometimes we'll make an iteration back to a previous increment if we learn that it's incorrect. And although we have, naturally, tested both the models and the mapping functions as we've gone along, we also need to test the final system to be delivered.

Formalizing Knowledge

Knowledge formalization comprises four activities:

- Gathering requirements relevant to the domain of interest
- Abstracting that knowledge into some set of concepts
- Expressing those concepts formally in a model
- Testing the model for correctness (preferably by executing it)

Gathering Requirements

Every subject matter area has a set of requirements placed upon it by its owners and users. A banking system, for example, may make loans, manage accounts, and charge customers for account usage monthly based on the number of transactions or the average minimum daily balance. Before any system can be built, the requirements must be gathered, understood, made consistent, and relieved of inconsistencies.

There are many ways to approach this work. We may employ use cases or user stories. We may build use case diagrams with stick figures, write a formalized document, or simply write text. If the system is small enough, we may use 3x5 cards to track each requirement, or simply do it verbally.

Regardless of whether you choose to gather most of your requirements initially or elect to gather them one by one, requirements need to be gathered together and communicated somehow.

Abstracting Solutions

Given a set of requirements, there are often many ways of abstracting a solution to the problem. Abstraction therefore involves wrapping one's mind around the many requirements and choosing to think about the solution in a particular way. For example, we may choose to think about accounts as the result of accumulated transactions, or we may choose to treat a transaction as the primary concept and the account as just the accumulated trace. This step tends not to receive the attention it deserves—it involves *thinking*.

Modeling

Once the analysts have selected an appropriate set of abstractions, the next step is to select a modeling language and/or a metamodel, and then build a model of these abstractions. This model describes and defines the abstracted concepts, and as such is a formalization of knowledge of the subject matter.

Testing the Model

Once the model has been constructed, the next step is to verify that the model is correct. In other words, you need to answer this question: Does the model do what you (your clients) want?

One approach to testing a model is to review it. Unfortunately, checking a model by hand is notoriously error-prone, and there's always the problem of multiple interpretations of the model by different people, especially if a broad metamodel is used. The alternative is to execute the models by generating test cases that set initial conditions and then providing some stimuli that cause the model to produce some output and to change the state of the system. These test cases may be derived more or less directly from the use cases or user stories.

Building Bridges

Building bridges also comprises four activities:

- Specifying mapping functions
- Marking the models
- Verifying the mappings
- Transforming the models

Specifying Mapping Functions

At this stage, on the one hand, we have a source model, and on the other, a target model that captures the abstractions that implement the concepts of the source model. The target model contains and formalizes knowledge about the target platform's structure and behavior. The problem now is to link these models together. We do this by specifying mapping functions, which we discussed in Chapter 5.

Once it's clear what the mapping is supposed to do, a mapping function implementor is faced with the following questions: How can a mapping function be specified such that it's easily extensible? What kind of notation should be used to express the mapping function specification? Can the concepts of MDA be applied to the specification of mapping functions by capturing the specifications in models and then using mapping functions to transform these models into executable implementations?

Interwoven with these issues about implementation techniques are questions regarding the particular details of the mapping output, such as, What are optimization criteria for target models, such as readability, style, aesthetics, efficiency, straightforward and recognizable mapping of source model concepts, and so forth?

As we pointed out in Chapter 5, the jury is still out as to which approach is best suited for expressing a mapping function.

Marking the Models

How did we know that an arbitrary source model entity should be persistent? In some cases, it may be possible to work this out analytically, but in the general case, we have to tell the system that *this* one is persistent but *that* one isn't. Hence, as we discussed in Chapter 6, we mark each model element in the source model to indicate that a particular mapping function must be used to determine the kind of associated target element we desire.

Assume that you have a source model (conforming to some metamodel, of course) and that you have selected a target model. In addition, you have a set of partial mapping functions, with their respective source and target marking models. We assume that these are partial, because if they were complete, the marking models would already be established, and there would be nothing to do. However, the mapping functions and marking models may be so incomplete as to be nonexistent, though as off-the-shelf models become more widespread, this will be less and less likely.

The task at hand is to ensure that an arbitrary conforming source model will map correctly into the selected target model. You may begin with any of the three inputs: a source metamodel, a target metamodel, or a set of mapping rules. We shall assume initially that you're going to start with the source metamodel.

In this case, the first part of the goal is simple: There must be at least one mapping rule for each model element. Note that the rule is from elements in the source metamodel to elements in the target model. This is because we don't care that you exercise every element type in the target metamodel, only that you can produce a correct target model for every possible conforming source model.

In limited circumstances, it's possible for the mapping from the source metamodel to have an incomplete mapping. For example, if your source model (*not* metamodel!) never makes use of delayed signals, there's no need to ensure there is a mapping for them. (Of course, if you choose this path, then continued vigilance will be required to ensure that no one ever uses delayed signals in the source model. See also Constraint Propagation and Verification in Chapter 11.)

The second part of the goal is to ensure that the mapping rule can be unambiguously selected. Mapping functions will often refer to input marking models that define marks to resolve ambiguities between mapping rules. If the choice of mapping rule is ambiguous, then you must add a discriminating mark to the marking model, and make the appropriate choice for each such ambiguity in the source model, which you'll do by adding marks in each case.

Once every element of the source metamodel has a mapping function, and every element of the source model has a mark or a default rule that unambiguously selects the mapping function, you have established your marking models completely.

Verifying the Mappings

After knowledge has been formalized in a model, and the model has been marked for its defined mapping functions, we must ensure that the combination of models and marks forms valid input for the mapping and that the mapping will produce valid results.

Consider a mapping that generates source code from a UML model. In the UML, it's perfectly fine to specify more than one generalization for one class, where those generalizations are also classes. The specification of more than one class as the generalization of another class can easily be mapped to the source code in C++. However, one can't use the same model to generate Java source code simply by putting the names of the generalizations into the "extends" clause of the class declaration, because Java allows only for single implementation inheritance. This source code would result in a compile error (better, of course, would be for the mapping function to take care of it).

This example demonstrates that the mapping function has to account for some source model constructs that cannot be translated plainly into target model constructs. You must make sure that there's a chain of mappings leading from the most abstract to the least abstract implementation-oriented metamodels. This is the only way to achieve a contiguous path along the mapping chain. Otherwise, knowledge formalized in one platform would be left untransformed on the way to the implementation, and this is undesirable for obvious reasons.

Once each element in the application model has a defined mapping function, execution of the mapping yields a PSM of the target system, as described below.

Transforming the Models

Transforming the models, like program compilation, is anticlimactic. Now that the models are marked, and we know that the mapping function specifications are complete, we can transform the formalized, marked, and verified knowledge into other models or source code comprising the system's implementation.

Note that model verification should occur every time before a mapping gets executed. This will help the team find and avoid errors as early as possible in the MDA process instead of deferring them to a later point.

An Example Model-Driven Process

As an example of a model-driven process with simple source and target models, consider our banking application with J2EE as its implementation platform. In this case, you will have to formalize the knowledge of the bank in a model, and then build a bridge from the Bank model to J2EE.

In general, of course, it's not quite as simple as having a single source model and a single preselected target implementation model. Rather, a typical system will comprise several platforms, and this means that there will be potentially several utilizations of the pair of high-level activities described above, not just one.

With these easily identified platforms on hand, you may also require other platforms for modeling at higher levels of abstraction. For this banking system, for example, you may identify the need for a platform on which the bank relies to ensure that certain operations can be carried out, and certain data accessed only by people playing certain authorized roles. If this behavior is formalized in a model of Security, then you will have to do the following:

- Formalize the knowledge of the bank in a model.
- Build a bridge from the Bank model to the Security model.
- Build bridges from the Bank and Security models to J2EE.

Each definition of the work to be done is the specification of a model-driven process for your particular project, given a particular set of platforms.

This model-driven process assumes the prior existence of the Security platform as a model. If, however, the Security platform doesn't exist, you'll have to build it by formalizing the knowledge of that subject matter. In that case, your process will be as follows:

- Formalize the knowledge of the bank in a model.
- Formalize the knowledge of security in a model.
- Build a bridge from the Bank model to the Security model.
- Build bridges from the Bank and Security models to J2EE.

The result of identifying these platforms and the bridges between them constitutes a specific model-driven process, the workflow if you like, for your project.

The overall structure of the process, then, is not only iterative and incremental, but also *recursive*. We formalize the knowledge for one platform and attempt to build a bridge to our platform's implementing abstractions. If that platform already exists, the mapping can proceed. If it doesn't, we must formalize the knowledge of the target platform before the mapping can be specified and executed.

Normally, of course, we plan ahead by searching out existing platforms and only build our own platforms from scratch when we have no choice. Many platforms near to the implementation will also already be realized. Examples include the Java platform; CORBA; .NET; operating systems like Linux, Solaris, and Windows; and specific real-time platforms.

Iterating the Process

If the platforms already exist, it's often the case that there may already be defined model-driven processes that can be used off the shelf. However, there will be cases in which the team has to adapt a model-driven process, for one reason or another, even while development is continuing. For example, if an architect on the project decides that a change in the target platform is necessary, then someone may have to change the bridge that creates the models for that platform. Ideally, though, the developers carrying out the model-driven process wouldn't even have to know, because they simply continue to formalize knowledge in each domain and build bridges, only applying the modified bridge for a given platform during the last step. Typically, this process will happen before the execution of the actual model-driven process.

After you've created your (customized) process, you can proceed by repeatedly applying the two high-level steps—knowledge formalization and building bridges—as suggested by the domain chart in Figure 11-1. As you go, you may have to adapt the process, by adapting some of the bridges, for example, or by changing platforms and their corresponding metamodels. In any case, you need to make sure that you lose as little of the formalized knowledge as possible.

Testing the System

The target model, if it's complete and ready for use on an executable platform, can now be executed. The behavior of the resulting system is the same as when the application model was tested at the end of the knowledge formalization step (assuming the mappings are specified correctly, of course).

The remaining testing work falls into two main categories. First, we have to make sure that the functions that the system performs are in compliance with the specification. Basically, these steps correspond with the normal testing routines that every software development process exhibits. Then, we must verify that the performance of the resulting system is adequate. If it isn't, it's likely that the choice of implementing abstractions, or the allocation implied by the marks, is at fault. Fixing these doesn't require any change to the application models, only to the implementing abstractions or annotations.

Executing an MDA Process

We execute the process as defined previously, taking into account all of the changes we had to make to the plan as we learned what the system was really about. A key feature of the process is the focus on both model building and the construction of transformations between them.

We can then deliver the system. And we're done! (Well...almost.)

Chapter 13

The Future of MDA

"Prediction is difficult," Yogi Berra is reported to have said, "especially about the future." And so it is, especially with the future of technology. Even so, we're willing to place our reputations in an unattended picnic basket and risk a look at the future of model-driven development.

The value proposition for MDA is that the cost of building and maintaining systems is significantly lower. The combination of the following makes a powerful business argument:

- Raising the level of abstraction so that people can express themselves and communicate with man and machine alike more productively
- Raising the level of reuse to a higher level of granularity so that bigger systems can be composed from ever-larger elements
- Relying on the power of design-time interoperability, so that models can stand alone, ready for combination with other models in an additive manner

Before we dive too deeply into speculation, however, we should be clear about where model-driven development is today. It is *not* just a vision: Many systems are being built using models, albeit not as many as we'd like, or as many as one might expect given the value proposition. Far too many folk are working at a lower, less-productive level of abstraction (read: "hacking code"). The question is, Why?

Why *Not* MDA?

One possible future, of course, is the failure of the concept of model-driven development in its entirety. Despite our trick of defining a program to be a model, the fact is that many people think of the code as the be-all-and-end-all of systems development, and that playing with pictures is only for kindergarten (the huge sums being made from stick-figure actors notwithstanding). If the code-is-all view prevails, MDA will be as dead as a ham sandwich.

Failure is a real possibility if MDA does not address the perception that models are "extra," that once you build a model and do with it what you will, then you have to write code and the model becomes superfluous. (This, remember, is what has caused the "extreme" backlash.) Models as blueprints, where models are intended to predict the construction of the system by hand, are the antithesis of MDA, yet that remains the perception.

To make models central to systems development, we need not only to address the technical issues (in other words, how to make MDA work), but also the sociological ones. Another point of possible failure is lack of acceptance by developers who fear for their jobs if coding skills become less important. The histories of many industries follow a pattern of increasing automation that reduces the overall employment in that sector. Why should software be any different?

It can also be argued that even if there is a job to be done, it would no longer be interesting. We would argue that automating model transformations is *not* about incapacitating software engineers; rather, it's about helping them build effective software efficiently.

The business of software engineers will evolve into expressing system functionality in models, metamodels, and mapping functions. This makes said engineers more efficient and rids them of uncreative tasks, just as compilers took away the drudgery—er, we mean, creativity—involved in making register allocations in function calls. However, that argument doesn't wash if the perception is otherwise. Compilers allowed us to build more complex systems and venture into new levels. Realizing the MDA vision will have a similar effect: It will lead to increasing specialization, which is a property of a maturing engineering discipline.

Bran Selic (2003) makes the case that the time is ripe for model-driven development because the technologies are maturing. He includes the ability to execute models, observe them in execution by tracing back to the models that generated them, scalability, and integration with existing systems. In addition to these key properties of the technology, Selic calls out the importance of standards, and the "network effect" they generate.

The Importance of Standards

The **network effect** is the notion that economies of scale grow exponentially as the number of nodes increases. The classic example is the telephone. One telephone on the planet is worthless; a hundred or a thousand, much better. Nowadays, area codes breed like rabbits, and people talk to themselves on the streets in a manner that would have caused them to be locked up only a few years ago. Perhaps less benign is the use of lowest-common-denominator tools "because everyone else uses them," even if the tools themselves don't inspire excitement. Four-letter model-building and word-processing tools spring to mind as examples.

Standards, with interchange and interoperability of course, mean that you can buy each of these tools from a different vendor, thus bypassing potentially monopolistic vendors who might otherwise become slothful. This allows you to pick the best tools for the job. The existing UML, QVT, and other MDA-related standards create the network effect because the existence of multiple vendors of standards-conforming tools reduces vendor "lock-in," the unhappy (for the buyer, that is) situation that you can only buy tools from a single vendor.

More standards will be required as MDA matures. These will address many technically detailed topics, such as standardization of metamodels; the use of UML profiles versus true meta-case tools that allow modelers to define their own graphical notations for their metamodels; and the standardization of mapping functions, platforms, and the architectures to which they map. There will be a need for the perfect integration of tools across all levels: an architecture construction kit, architecture wizards that help us find and experiment with different architectures. "What kind of persistence mechanism would you like to use—a relational DB, OODB, file, hierarchical, host-based? What component framework would you like on top—J2EE, .NET, none? What type of front end would you like to build—Web-based, 3270, fat client?" Damn! There's that animated paper clip again!

Model-driven *architecture*, of course, is the name of the game. Not only must there be standards for the UML, the MOF, QVT, and all of the rest, but it's also critically important that tools built to these standards also fit together within that architecture and so create a complete model-driven development environment. This set of tools, loosely sequenced, constitutes a **tool chain.** MDA intends to build the architecture for this tool chain.

Building a Tool Chain

There are many possible tools that need to be integrated to make a complete development environment. In this book alone, we have suggested the need for model builders, mapping function tools, model compilers, and so forth.

With the right standards, one can envision tools that do the following:

- Transform one representation of the same underlying model to another representation friendlier to a reader
- Generate test vectors against the model, and then run them
- Check for state-space completeness, decidability, reachability, and the like
- Manage deployment into processors, hardware, software, and firmware
- Mark models
- Partition or combine behavior models for visualization or deployment
- Analyze performance against a given deployment
- Examine the generated code in execution (in other words, model debuggers)

We can imagine a developer receiving a model from a vendor or colleague; turning that model into a comfy notation or format; making a change with a model builder; verifying that the behavior is correct by analysis and by running test cases; marking the models and deploying them; analyzing performance; debugging the resulting system, and so forth.

Note that this list of tool ideas sounds exactly like what we have with modern source code IDEs. None of this is necessarily specific to MDA. The needs we know from the 3GL tool world, by the same rationale, also apply to the MDA world. Models can capture design information that's normally lost in the code, so that tools, such as analyzers, test generation tools, and so forth can be more effective than they are today with 3GL tools.

When developers have the ability to provide specification tidbits at varying levels of abstraction and then link them all together, MDA will face additional tool challenges regarding smooth integration between different specification levels, such as consistency checking, constraint propagation, and incremental mapping function execution. This will, admittedly, be trickier than it is in a 3GL world.

Working with Models-as-Assets

Models-as-assets change how we work as software developers. Just as thirty years ago, developers learned to relax, forget about register allocation, and love programming language compilers that conferred hardware-platform independence, so too will we learn to relax, forget about distribution, and love model compilers that confer independence from the software platform.

We can therefore look forward to the day when software developers search the Web for reusable models that have the required functionality, and then combine those models with model compilers that deliver the appropriate per-formance for the event rates and data access patterns—which can, in turn, be combined with common infrastructure for the enterprise. Subset the models, add a little functionality perhaps, and away we go.

The incremental cost will reside primarily in selecting the appropriate models and linking them together. The models themselves will need to be con-structed, of course, but once they're complete, they will have greater longev-ity than code because they will evolve independently of other models.

We developers will not hack out code, or even models. Rather, we will do the following:

- Develop and define the MDA process to be used.
- Take a model of an application subject matter off the shelf.
- Subset the model as necessary.
- Take models of the implementation technologies off the shelf.
- Describe how the models are to be linked.

- Mark the source models.
- Generate the system.

When it comes time to change the application, we will make the changes in the application model, marks, or mapping functions, as appropriate, and leave the models of the implementation technologies alone. When we need to retarget an application to a different implementation environment, we will select the models for the new environment and regenerate. There will be no need to modify the application models. Costs will be lower; productivity will be higher, based on increased reuse of models; maintenance will be cheaper—and each new UML model that's built will become an asset that can be subsequently reused.

Note that this vision is already a reality in the hardware world. Hardware designers already have online libraries where vendors offer designs for sale. These designs constitute valuable (and, controversially, protectable) intellectual property.

Beyond UML

In the best of all possible worlds, no one writes software any more. Instead, users, not developers, describe desired behavior formally using a language specific to their subject matter. Control engineers, for example, would use control diagrams, while manufacturing plant operators would describe the desired sequence of operations to be carried out in a visual language of their own devising. Accountants would think accounting; lawyers would think about, well, their fees.

This vision does require users to have some abstraction capability. Just as today, such skills will likely be in short supply, but the level of the domain-specific language would be high enough that the semantic gap between domain concepts and the language would be low. This is not as farfetched as it sounds: Spreadsheets do just that. Such a future would make UML an unnecessary evil. Instead, subject-matter experts would work with domain-specific visual languages—tied in with the MDA infrastructure, of course— in which they themselves "program," relying on MDA infrastructure to deliver an implementation.

Note that this moves away from MDA's focus on infrastructure. Once that infrastructure is constructed, the variability in subject matter will be much greater, and much more interesting, than variability in platforms (just as there are more frameworks and models than compilers today). In addition to the economy of scale that comes from the network effect, we also get an economy of scope due to the enormous number of model combination possibilities—plus the fact that a small model delta can be additively combined with all the other existing models, so that a relatively small input creates a great variety. This eventually enables mass customization.

This is where system families play an important role in shifting the focus from thinking about platform independence to breaking up and scoping subject matters from application domains to achieve these economies of scope. Understandably, MDA currently focuses on getting the basic implementation technology standards done. However, systematic ways to scope and select domains, and to develop and manage domain-specific languages, will eventually be much more important. MDA inevitably enables a move in that direction.

Back from the Future

But that's in the future. For now, MDA is a broad umbrella that covers a set of related technologies—all modeling standards adopted by the OMG—that support design-time interoperability. It provides companies that adopt it with the ability to derive code from a set of stable models as the underlying infrastructure shifts over time, and with a healthy return on investment from reuse of domain models across the life span of software.

In the final analysis, though, we must remember the words of Hannah Arendt (Arendt 1972), a German-born U.S. political philosopher who said:

> *Predictions of the future are never anything but projections of present automatic processes and procedures, that is, of occurrences that are likely to come to pass if men do not act and if nothing unexpected happens; every action, for better or worse, and every accident necessarily destroys the whole pattern in whose frame the prediction moves and where it finds its evidence.*

It's up to you where MDA goes.

Glossary

abstracting mapping A *mapping* that intentionally omits information contained in a more concrete *model* that's considered irrelevant detail in the more abstract model.

abstraction A *modeling* technique that involves ignoring information that is not of interest in a particular context. Abstraction involves choosing how to think about a problem and its solution, which also requires creativity and analysis.

abstraction hierarchy A graph within which the nodes are *metamodels* that factor out all commonalities of the subject matters from which they abstract.

abstract syntax The structure of a language separate from its concrete notational symbols.

agile MDA An approach in which *models* are linked together and then mapped to a single combined model that is then translated into code according to a single system architecture.

bridge At construction time, the combination of *mapping functions*, *marks*, and *marking models* that serves to link two *models* together.

classification A *modeling* technique that involves grouping important information based on common properties, even though the things under study are, of course, different from one another.

composed realization A realization of a *platform* that's comprised of one or more other realizations.

constraint A specification of a condition that must hold true in order for a *model* to be "well-formed."

design-time interoperability The type of interoperability that is achieved when gluing the various layers of *abstraction* together and combining models is deferred to the last minute during design.

domain chart A diagram that shows *problem domains* and the *bridges* among those domains.

entity bean An object that can live for the lifetime of the software system and whose state is stored in and loaded from an underlying database.

executable model A *model* that is complete in that it has everything required to produce the desired functionality of a single *problem domain*.

Executable UML A UML *profile* that defines an execution semantics for a carefully selected streamlined subset of the UML.

generalization A relationship between a general class (the superclass or parent) and a more specific version of that class (the subclass or child).

horizontal mapping A *mapping* that results in a target *model* at the same level of subject-matter *abstraction* as the level at which the source model resides.

invariant A condition that must hold true for all instances of a particular *model* element (such as all objects that belong to a given class).

join point A correspondence between a *problem domain* that is created and maintained separately from the *model* of that domain.

long-hop mapping A *mapping* that results in a significant change in abstraction level between the source *model* and the target model.

M0 layer The layer in the four-level *metamodel* hierarchy that contains the data of the application (for example, the instances populating an object-oriented system at runtime, or rows in relational database tables).

M1 layer The layer in the four-level *metamodel* hierarchy that contains the *metadata* of the application (for example, the classes of an object-oriented system, or the table definitions of a relational database).

M2 layer The layer in the four-level *metamodel* hierarchy that contains the metametadata that describes the properties that metadata may exhibit (for example, UML elements such as Class, Attribute, and Operation).

M3 layer The layer in the four-level *metamodel* hierarchy that contains metametametadata that describes the properties that metametadata can exhibit.

mapping The application or execution of a *mapping function* in order to transform one *model* to another.

mapping chain Two or more *mappings* linked together, where the outputs of one mapping serve as the inputs for another mapping.

mapping function A collection of *mapping rules* that defines how a particular *mapping* works.

mapping rule A rule that describes one aspect of how a *mapping function* works.

mark A lightweight, nonintrusive extension to a *model* that captures information required for model transformation without polluting that model.

marking model A *model* that defines the structure of, and types for, a set of *marks*, as well as default values and rules that construct default values when a value for a mark is absent.

MDA See *model-driven architecture (MDA)*.

MDA process A specific process that one applies on an *MDA* project.

merge conflict A collision between two or more changes to a common element, usually requiring human intervention to resolve.

merging mapping A *mapping* that combines more than one source *model* into a single target model.

metadata Data about data.

metamodel A *model* that defines the structure, semantics, and constraints for a family of models.

Meta-Object Facility (MOF) A language that defines a set of *modeling* constructs that a modeler can use to define and manipulate a set of interoperable *metamodels*.

migrating mapping A *mapping* that results in a target *model* expressed in a different form from the source model.

model A simplification of something so we can view, manipulate, and reason about it, and so help understand the complexity inherent in the subject under study.

model compiler A tool that takes a set of *Executable UML models* and weaves them together according to a consistent set of rules.

model-driven architecture (MDA) A set of technologies and techniques that enable model-driven development.

model elaboration The idea that a target *model* can be modified after it has been generated.

MOF See *Meta-Object Facility (MOF)*.

Object Constraint Language (OCL) A formal language that *modelers* can use to express conditions that must hold true for the system being modeled.

OCL See *Object Constraint Language (OCL)*.

PIM See *platform-independent model (PIM)*.

platform The specification of an execution environment for a set of *models*.

platform-independent model (PIM) A *model* of a subject matter whose metamodel represents abstractions from one or more *platform* models.

platform-specific model (PSM) A *model* that incorporates details about *platforms*.

postcondition A condition that must hold true at the moment that execution of an operation has just ended.

precondition A condition that must hold true at the moment that execution of a particular operation is about to begin.

primitive realization A realization of a *platform* that stands on its own.

problem domain A subject matter that can be understood independently of other subject matters.

profile A UML mechanism for adapting an existing *metamodel* with constructs that are specific to a particular domain, *platform*, or method.

PSM See *platform-specific model (PSM)*.

refining mapping A *mapping* that allows the modeler to express detail in the target *model* that doesn't apply in the more abstract source model.

representing mapping A *mapping* that allows the representation of a *model* to be edited and the changes mapped back to the original model.

session bean An object with state that is transaction-aware and lives for the life of a client session.

short-hop mapping A *mapping* that results in a small change in *abstraction* level between the source *model* and the target model.

stateful session bean An object that lives for the life of a client session.

stereotype Something that extends the basic vocabulary of the UML.

tagged value Something that extends the properties of an element of a UML *model*, but not instances of that element.

type A group of *model* elements with common properties.

vertical mapping A *mapping* that results in a target *model* at a different level of subject-matter *abstraction* than the level at which the source model resides.

well-formedness rule A rule that specifies a condition that a *model* must satisfy in order to be "well-formed."

XMI See *XML Model Interchange (XMI)*.

XML Model Interchange (XMI) A protocol that defines rules for deriving an XML Document Type Definition (DTD) from a MOF-compliant modeling language as well as rules for rendering a compliant model into a compliant XML document.

Bibliography

Arendt, Hannah. "On Violence," sect. 1, from *Crises of the Republic.* Orlando, Florida: Harcourt Brace & Company, 1972.

Atkinson, Colin and Thomas Kühne. "Model-Driven Development: A Metamodeling Foundation," *IEEE Software,* September/October 2003.

Beck, Kent. *Extreme Programming Explained.* Boston, MA: Addison Wesley, 2000.

Bock, Conrad. "UML without Pictures," *IEEE Software*, September/October 2003.

Frankel, David S. *Model Driven Architecture: Applying MDA to Enterprise Computing.* Indianapolis, IN: John Wiley & Sons, 2003.

Garlan, David, R. Allen, and J. Ockerbloom: "Architectural Mismatch: Why Reuse Is So Hard," *IEEE Software*, 12(6): 17-26, 1994.

Kleppe, Anneke, Jos Warmer, and Wim Bast. *MDA Explained: The Model Driven Architecture—Practice and Promise.* Boston, MA: Addison-Wesley, 2003.

Mellor, Stephen J. and Marc J. Balcer. *Executable UML: A Foundation for Model-Driven Architecture.* Boston, MA: Addison-Wesley, 2002.

Object Management Group. Human Usable Textual Notation, revised submission, 1 April 2002; *www.omg.org/cgi-bin/doc?ad/2002-03-02.*

Object Management Group. "Model Driven Architecture," white paper, Draft 3.2, November 2000; *ftp://ftp.omg.org/pub/docs/omg/00-11-05.pdf.*

Object Management Group. *Unified Modeling Language: Superstructure.* Version 2.0, ptc/03-07-06, July 2003; *http://www.omg.org/cgi-bin/doc?ptc/ 2003-08-02.*

Selic, Bran. "The Pragmatics of Model-Driven Development," *IEEE Software*, September/October 2003.

Stachowiak, Herbert. *Allgemeine Modelltheorie*. Vienna, Austria: Springer-Verlag, 1973.

Weis, Torben, Andreas Ulbrich, and Kurt Giehs. "Model Metamorphosis," *IEEE Software,* September/October 2003.

Index

INDEX 149

We build software standards that work,

and work,

and work,

and work,

and work,

and work,

and work,

and work,

and work,

and work,

and work,

and work,

and work,

and work,

These days, you need software standards that work for you. Standards that don't hem you in. Standards that simplify inter-operability, allowing you to integrate easily a variety of technologies. Standards that enhance the stability of your infrastructure, while reducing your total cost of ownership. Standards that help you meet the constantly changing needs of the enterprise, quickly and cost-effectively. Open standards, based on an open process.

Object Management Group and its members have delivered those standards for more than a decade. Thousands of enterprises around the world have leveraged OMG standards to create the interoperable enterprise applications that are shaping the way companies work and communicate. They've chosen OMG open standards for one simple reason: They work.

Model Driven Architecture™ at work.

OMG's Model Driven Architecture (MDA™) provides a comprehensive interoperability architecture that embraces evolving standards and technologies.

Based on well-established OMG standards, MDA accelerates development of new applications, simplifies integration with existing technology and reduces costs throughout the application lifecycle.

MDA is working for a large government system handling 30,000 database hits per minute, yielding cost savings of 65% for coding and 26% for the entire project.

Unified Modeling Language™ at work.

OMG's Unified Modeling Language (UML™) enables system architects to specify, visualize and document models of distributed software systems to meet real-world business requirements. UML enhances application scalability, robustness, and security, while promoting efficient code re-use.

UML works for a major international airline, capturing user requirements, defining design, and generating documentation for a 3-tier flight-crew scheduling application written in Java, C++, and SQL by an international development team.

CORBA™ at work.

Since its introduction in 1991, CORBA (Common Object Request Broker Architecture) has become the middleware of choice for companies seeking an open, vendor-independent specification that enables heterogeneous systems and applications to work together over networks.

CORBA works for a major medical benefits provider, linking databases on multiple platforms including some acquired companies, to service 47 million patients referred and paid by 10,000 different plan sponsors.

Who's working for you?

Why put your future in the hands of vendors with closed technology? Take control of your own software destiny. Join the 600-plus companies participating in the open OMG consortium collaborating on the enterprise standards that are working to give them a competitive edge.

To learn more, or to join OMG, call us at (781) 444-0404 or visit us today at www.omg.org.

OBJECT MANAGEMENT GROUP

Register
Your Book

at www.awprofessional.com/register

You may be eligible to receive:

- Advance notice of forthcoming editions of the book
- Related book recommendations
- Chapter excerpts and supplements of forthcoming titles
- Information about special contests and promotions throughout the year
- Notices and reminders about author appearances, tradeshows, and online chats with special guests

Contact us

If you are interested in writing a book or reviewing manuscripts prior to publication, please write to us at:

Editorial Department
Addison-Wesley Professional
75 Arlington Street, Suite 300
Boston, MA 02116 USA
Email: AWPro@aw.com

Addison-Wesley

Visit us on the Web: http://www.awprofessional.com